Cover photo. The author in the early 1980's about to go on the air live with a report of the visit to Hunstville, Alabama of two astronauts from a Space Shuttle mission.

Back Cover photo. From 2011, the author holding a moon rock brought back to earth during one of the NASA missions to the moon.

Other books by Steve Newvine

9 FROM 99-Experiences from California's Central Valley

SOFT SKILLS IN HARD TIMES

GROWING UP, UPSTATE

TEN MINUTES TO AIR

GO WHERE YOU'RE NEEDED

Microphones, Moon Rocks, and Memories

Columns, book excerpts, and new writings

By Steve Newvine

Copyright 2011 by Steve Newvine

All rights reserved.

No part of this book may be reprinted without the written consent of the author. No part of this publication may be reproduced, stored in or introduced into a retrieval system such as Google Books, or transmitted, in any form, or by any means without the prior written permission of the author.

All photos are from the author with the exception of Junior Achievement (Business Education Alliance of Merced) and Rick Krolak (RickKrolak.com).

Opinions expressed here are solely those of the author Steve Newvine. Characters, events, and descriptions in the fictional essays are from the author's imagination. Any similarities to real people are entirely coincidental.

Microphones, Moon Rocks, and Memories

Columns, book excerpts, and new writings

By Steve Newvine

CONTENTS

Section 1 - Microphones   *11*

1. Community Radio (fiction)
2. My First Job in Television News
3. Rotary Corn Festival

Section 2 - Celebrities   *23*

4. Jack Benny
5. Jack and Johnny
6. Johnny Carson
7. Andy Rooney
8. Drew Carey and Bill Cullen
9. Susanne Pleshette

Section 3 - Personal Development   *41*

10. Katie Couric and Comfort Zones
11. Volunteering and George
12. The Commencement Speech
13. Marriage
14. The Apology

Section 4 - Moon Rocks   *57*

15. Moon Rocks
16. Apollo 11 Anniversary
17. The End of the Shuttle Program

Section 5 - Growing Up   *71*

18. 1968
19. The End of Pontiac
20. The Edison
21. Joe Dunn's Dry Goods Store
22. My Years as an Altar Boy

Section 6 - Passings   *87*

23. Rick Krolak
24. Robert B. Parker
25. Steve Jobs

Section 7 - Holidays   *97*

26. Christmas at the Convent
27. Thanksgiving
28. Christmas Music

Section 8 - Hodge Podge for $40   *105*

29. Reflections on Two Inaugurations
30. Watson and the Gut Instinct
31. Operation Power Flite
32. Junior Achievement
33. A Friendship Forged In Radio
34. Grief Ministry with a Nine Iron
35. September 11 at Ten

Dedication

To the people who offered me jobs throughout my working life: Dave, Mark, Mike, Dick, Gil, Scott, Joe, Kathy, a different Mark, and Mary. It can only happen when someone says, "You're hired."

Special Thanks

I thank the editors at several newspapers across the country for publishing my columns over the years including the *Merced Sun Star* who graciously allowed me to republish some of my essays here. I also thank Brad Haven from *MercedCountyEvents.com* for giving me a writing home during 2011.

Introduction

I've been writing on and off professionally for over thirty years. The first fifteen of those years I was a television journalist working for stations in Binghamton (NY), Hunstville (AL), Rockford (IL), and Rochester (NY). After that, I moved into association management where my duties included writing and editing the organization's monthly newsletter. In my job now as an energy analyst, I write a monthly update (the new generation name for a newsletter).

The first time I submitted something (other than an occasional letter to the editor) to a newspaper for publication was in the late 1980's when I answered a call from our Diocesan newspaper for essays on special Christmas memories. The essay formed the basis for a short story I wrote over twenty years later called *Go Where You're Needed*.

When my broadcast news hero David Brinkley passed away in 2003, I wrote an appreciation of his work for the *Rochester Democrat and Chronicle*. It was published on their opinion and editorial pages (known also as op/ed page). From that point forward, I managed to write something along the lines of an op/ed or a column about three to four times a year. In addition to the Rochester newspaper, my essays have been published in such cities as Binghamton (NY), Fresno (CA), and Merced (CA).

In 2005, I wrote a chapter for a book on one of my favorite comedians, Jack Benny. The book, *Well! Reflections on the Life and Career of Jack Benny* is still available through Amazon. My chapter centers on the famous comedian's long time friendship with Johnny Carson.

In 2007, I started an annual tradition of writing a book. Using advice from my English teachers at South Lewis High School, I wrote about "something I knew". My first book was *Growing Up, Upstate* about my years as a child and adolescent in Port Leyden, New York. I followed that book the next year with the previously mentioned *Go Where You're Needed*. Then there was the murder mystery *Ten Minutes to Air*, a personal development guide *Soft Skills for Hard Times*, and my book about my first seven years in the Golden State called *9 From 99- Experiences in California's Central Valley*.

While I enjoy writing books, I appreciate the discipline involved with the writing of a column for a newspaper. When webmaster Brad Haven from the *website MercedCountyEvents.com* approached me in 2011 about doing a column twice a month, I accepted the opportunity. Writing to a deadline is a challenge and one that I am proud to take on.

What follows are some of the columns I've written for the website, selected opinion pieces that ran in newspapers (with updates where appropriate), a sampling from the books I've written, and new work.

Steve Newvine
SteveNewvine@sbcglobal.net
2011

Section 1 Microphones

I think I knew sometime around the age of three that my life's work might include holding a microphone. That's when I would stand behind my mom's record cabinet and pretend I was Hugh Downs hosting the game show *Concentration*. My bathrobe was my suit coat for these pretend hosting jobs. What follows are essays that center on my work as a television journalist as well as one essay on the night I held the microphone at a community concert.

1

Community Radio- from *Sign On at Sunrise* (fiction)

I hope to release Sign On at Sunrise in 2013. It's a novel about a teenager who gets a job as a disk jockey at a local radio station in upstate New York during the mid 1970's.

With his first weekend under his belt, Grey was adjusting to his new job at daytime radio station WTHR. It was the perfect spot for a first year college student. He now had a part time job in the field he had chosen for a career.

He could manage the commute to his parents' house on weekends. Tug Hill Community College was about an hour's drive from Grey's hometown. His plan was to stay on-campus during the week and drive back home for his weekend radio job. He barely broke even stretching his income from the weekend radio work to cover his expenses maintaining a car. But he was gaining experience in a real radio station.

As a cold and snowy winter eventually worked its' way to a warm and rainy spring, Grey's routine was refined. He usually stayed near the campus on Friday nights to enjoy some of what college students were doing socially. On Saturday, he would drive to his home to visit his parents, get his laundry done, and help out around the house. On Sunday, it was all about getting to the radio station for his shift as an announcer.

Whenever he had a break from college, he'd go to the station to watch the other announcers do their shows. Each announcer had a unique way of running their audio board, handling phone calls, preparing for newscasts, and doing their FCC required meter readings.

Senior announcer and morning personality Ron Donaldson was the master. Not only did he have the personable on-air presence, he also could do all the tasks necessary to keep his show running smoothly while taking on a few extra tasks. Among the extras Ron could master was producing a commercial while he playing a record on the air. Most announcers would have about an hour of production duties before or after their on-air shift during a typical broadcast workday. Production duties included producing commercials. Ron did a standard production shift, but if pressed for time, he could pull together a commercial production while maintaining a live program.

As they were closer in age, Grey found himself observing Randy Litford more than the others.

Randy definitely had a unique way of approaching his work. He'd show up about a half-hour before his on-air shift and prepare what would become the first half-hour of his show. He'd pull records from the play list rack and stack them alongside a legal note pad. Then, he'd check the wire service and pull the latest sports and weather forecasts so that he'd have the copy near him while on the air. He'd also review the national news wire to determine whether there might be some pronunciation challenges he needed to work through before reading the news.

It was obvious to Grey why Randy prepared his first half hour of his program so thoroughly. Once Randy's *All Request* program started, he would be on the phone constantly taking requests from listeners. Grey knew he wouldn't have much time to ask questions of his mentor, but he was learning a lot just watching him.

The play list wasn't so much a piece of paper with a list of songs as it was a storage area for the records the station wanted to be played frequently. Stored in what appeared to be an old dresser drawer with slats separating the various categories, the play list area could hold well over two hundred 45-RPM records. The categories included: country, easy listening, rock, instrumentals, and "OH". In the "OH" bin were a mix of rock and country songs including *Stairway to Heaven* and Red Sovine's *Teddy Bear*. Grey asked Randy what "OH" meant.

"Outhouse," came the reply. "These are songs that are at least five-minutes long. When you're working alone, there will come a time when you may need to play one of these."

With that, Grey picked up another lesson in this fascinating new world called community radio.

Mark Williams and Steve at WICZ-TV in 1979
(Steve Newvine personal collection)

2

My First Job in Television News

From MercedCountyEvents.com, this column is based on a photograph taken during my first paying job as a television journalist.

My Webmaster Brad Haven is always challenging me to provide a picture with my columns. He has explained to me how a picture can help illuminate a point. He has even sent me an article about how a picture is worth more than a thousand words. He's right. Pictures definitely help when you're trying to tell a story.

I believe I have found another reason to look for a photograph to accompany each of my columns. So taking Brad's advice from early in this assignment, I went back to my photographs.

When you encounter writer's block, go to the pictures. And that's what leads me to this photograph I found in my career scrapbook the other day.

The photo shows a very young Steve Newvine (on the right) trying to write a television news story from the newsroom at WICZ-TV in Binghamton, New York. The year was 1979. The man on the left was my first television news boss Mark Williams. Mark had been elevated to News Director only a couple of months prior to the time this photograph was taken. I was his first hire.

Fresh out of college (Syracuse University) I interviewed for the job during my finals. I remember not being so sure I impressed him in the interview, but I had an audition tape (a video tape of stories I produced while at a college internship at another TV station). Mark saw enough potential there is put me on his short list. He promised to get back to me by the end of the week.

He called me again on a Thursday night and said he had to run a few things past his general manager. He said he would call me Friday. I hung up the phone, announced to my parents that I wouldn't be going to sleep that night as I worried about whether I would actually be offered the job.

I did fall asleep later that night (probably early in the morning of that Friday). I stayed close to the phone all day Friday. At six-thirty PM, someone in my family suggested I go outside for a walk. I resigned myself to thinking that maybe Mark got caught up in his work of the week. I refused to think he might have changed his mind.

I put on my sneakers and headed out the door.

Then the phone rang. It was Mark. He offered me the job. I accepted. He asked when I could start, and I said "Monday!" We wished each other a good weekend. I hung up the phone, hugged my family, and started packing for Binghamton.

I said my goodbyes to my relatives, withdrew my life savings up to that point (about $500), and left for my first paying job in television news that weekend.

As the picture shows, I reported and wrote news for the station. Mark and I, along with four or five other staff people, made up the news department. We had no state or national wire service. Mark had a lot of contacts throughout the viewing area that he routinely called to get tips on potential local news stories. I learned from him and the others how to produce a news story, how to assemble an entire newscast, how to shoot video when my photographer couldn't accompany me on a story, and how to connect with the local community.

During my year and a half at WICZ-TV, I did every on-air job the station had including news, weather, sports, talk show host, and outdoors sports reporter. Station finances in 1980 forced a layoff that spared my job, but sent a chilling message to everyone that we better cover our bets and prepare for even tougher times. I started looking for a new job shortly after returning from my honeymoon in July. In

October, I left the station for WAAY-TV in Hunstville, Alabama. I stayed in television news for another fourteen years.

I'm glad I found that old picture from thirty-two years ago in my scrapbook. I exchange an occasional email from the man who hired me. Some of the radio and television broadcasters in the Binghamton market have formed a reunion club. They host a dinner and awards event every year. One of these days, I'm going to attend.

You never forget your first job. I had lots of jobs throughout high school and college that helped pay college costs and other expenses, but the first job in the field that I trained for will always remain a special memory.

And I have a picture to remind me of just how special that time was.

On stage at the Avon Rotary Corn Festival concert
(Steve Newvine personal collection)

3

Behind the Microphone at the Rotary Corn Festival

Long after I gave up the professional microphone for a career in chamber of commerce management, I still couldn't take myself away from microphones. This is from MercedCountyEvents.com and a more localized version that ran in the Avon Rotary Corn Festival program. It takes me back to the time when we lived in Western New York and I had the honor of serving as President of my local Rotary Club.

The Rotary Club I belonged to in Avon, New York celebrated the twenty-fifth anniversary of a summer festival that has put the community on the map.

The Avon Corn Festival provides entertainment, arts, and (you guessed it) corn to tens of thousands of visitors over the past two and a half decades. The Avon Rotary Club sponsors the event, but it really belongs to the entire community.

The idea for a Corn Festival began when interested citizens met to brainstorm ideas for some kind of event to celebrate the community's agricultural heritage. Some civic clubs and community members grabbed onto the idea of a festival named after a popular local crop and made their idea happen in 1987. In the early years, the festival experienced some growing pains. But one organization, Avon Rotary Club, hung in there and continues to present the event every year on the first Saturday in August.

As a member of the club, my memories include the several weeks of preparation, an intense week leading up to the festival, and an extremely long day when the festival actually arrived.

Year after year, the festival defined summertime in that small upstate New York community. One year it rained practically all day. We had company visiting and thought their first exposure to the festival would have to wait until another year. Later in the day, the rain stopped and we took a walk to the festival grounds where I saw one of the largest crowds ever. It seemed the entire community wouldn't let the rain spoil their event.

I joined the Avon Rotary Club in 1995 and was elected President five years later. One of my duties as President was to welcome the community to a free rock and roll concert to cap the full day of activities.

Having never met a microphone I didn't like, I fell into the role nicely. I walked up to the stage, adjusted the microphone stand, and thanked everyone for helping our club make the event a success. I kept it short, as I knew the crowd wasn't there to see me. I felt like a cross between Dick Clark and Ryan Secrest as I introduced the band called the *Skycoasters!*

There would be a lot of hard work the day and night of the festival, but our job was far from over. The next morning, every Rotarian was expected to be back at the festival site to take down any remaining booths and tents, as well as to sweep the streets and get the area looking better than we found it just two days prior.

I have spoken and written about this community's celebration of agriculture to groups in New York, Delaware, and here in California. I speak to groups about how a small village in upstate New York could create a powerful tourism venue. I've written about Avon Rotary's fund raising event in a book on personal development skills *Soft Skills in Hard Times*. My message is simple: find something that makes your town unique, mobilize your community's energy through volunteers, and promote the heck out of it.

It was a privilege serving in Avon Rotary for ten of the twenty years I lived in that community. My proudest moment during that time was sponsoring a member who would eventually become President of the Club. Being part of the Corn Festival was truly the most rewarding aspect of my time with Rotary. Everyone in the Club knew that a successful festival would help the Club give back to so many community organizations and charitable causes.

In twenty-five years, that single focus has never changed!

Section 2- Celebrities

I've met more than a fair share of celebrities over the past thirty-two years. George H.W. Bush shook my hand and posed for a picture (but my camera ran out of film). Jerry Lewis answered my question at a news conference about a book he was writing on the Dean Martin partnership. I have met about a half dozen astronauts including Apollo 13's Jim Lovell. All were fascinating. But there are few I have never met who are special.

4

Jack Benny

A guest column published in the Rochester Democrat and Chronicle in May 2007 inspired this essay. I have removed local references and a time sensitive news development since the first publication.

It was a true milestone in the history of radio broadcasting.

May 2, 1932 was the date of the first broadcast of the Jack Benny radio program. That accomplishment will probably go unnoticed these days. What a shame.

The Jack Benny radio program ran for thirty-three seasons with well over six hundred broadcasts. Fans and scholars cite many reasons for the sustained success of the Benny program.

The supporting cast of characters, each with a distinct public personality, allowed the writers to shift the laughs and the pressure to "carry the show" away from the star. Whether it was the wise cracking girl pal Mary Livingstone (Benny's real life wife), rotund announcer Don Wilson, band-leader and resident drinker Phil Harris, or legendary doofus Dennis Day, the show had several support beams to build on an already strong foundation. Benny, as supervisor of the writing team, encouraged the sharing of the spotlight by reminding his writers that if the audience found the show funny, they found the "Benny show" funny.

Benny's writers created a persona for the star that gave the show an instant following. The writers would have you believe Jack was cheap, vain, wore bad toupees, and fashioned himself a ladies man. None of these character traits were true (with the possible exception of the toupees). But the audience was in on the gag and it worked week after week.

As he aged, he embraced television. His weekly television program ran for sixteen years, with the first five years alternating every other week while he kept the radio series going on a weekly basis. His TV show was cancelled by CBS in the early 1960's, and moved for one final season to NBC. He continued showing up as a guest on variety shows and an occasional special until his death in 1974 at the age of 80.

Television stars such as Johnny Carson and Bob Newhart have frequently mentioned Benny as an influence. Carson's single camera leer emulates Benny's legendary stare into the camera. David Letterman and Regis Philbin do the same thing today.

Listening to successful morning radio teams you can hear the formulas that had their start in the Benny era. These shows have supporting players. Whether they are the news anchors, weather casters or traffic reporters, they play off the main team and have their Genesis in the supporting player concept popularized by the Benny program.

It's hard to imagine a time when radio was a truly important and positive influence in our lives. Jack Benny popularized the medium, and influenced American life in a many ways.

Jack Benny was a gentleman. His legacy was one of nice guys finishing first. His radio career shouldn't go unnoticed. American radio needs him now more than ever.

5

Jack and Johnny

Steve was among a dozen writers and fans of comedian Jack Benny contributed to this compilation edited by Michael Lennah in 2006. The book is available at Amazon.com, Oldies.com, and BearManorMedia.com

This is a condensed version of the chapter I wrote for the book Well! Reflections on the Life and Career of Jack Benny (Edited by Michael Lennah, Bear Manor Publishing)

Jack Benny's fan base extended to the baby boom generation in a big way. Many of us became fans as we watched the final years of his weekly TV shows in the early 1960's, or watched his annual specials during his "comedian emeritus" career stage in the late 60's and early 70's. As a young boy growing up in Port Leyden, New York in the 1960's, I became a Jack Benny fan in part due to the relationship Jack had with Johnny Carson.

I have memories of watching Jack Benny on Sunday nights in the early 1960's. When the show moved to a later time on a Tuesday night my viewing was compromised by parents who adhered to a strict school night bedtime schedule for my brother, my sister, and me. During that period, I got my Benny fixes through his guest appearances on other star's programs or by watching Jack's show during school vacations. Thankfully for me, the final season of the weekly Benny program was broadcast on Friday nights.

After that season, I enjoyed Jack's specials as I became aware of another comedian who was making his mark in late night television.

I became a Johnny Carson fan shortly after I convinced my mother to let me stay up real late on Friday nights to watch *The Tonight Show Starring Johnny Carson.* In those pre VCR days, this was the best I could hope for. If I could stay awake through the late news, I knew I would be good for until Johnny's ninety-minute show ended at 1:00 am. It was only a matter of time before I got Mom to let me watch Johnny regularly during school vacations. Watching Johnny was cool for a junior high school aged young man.

A DVD of Johnny's early network TV work includes his first appearance on Jack's TV show. The broadcast is dated 1955 although the Irving Fein biography of Jack says that appearance took place three years earlier. It's clear from the video of this appearance that Jack liked the young Nebraskan almost as much as the boyish star-to-be admired and appreciated his idol.

Of his young guest, Jack previews the appearance by telling the audience, "This fellow has everything it takes to be a success."

Johnny takes the stage at CBS Television City clearly in awe of his new friend. The pair works through a routine where Jack allows Johnny to critique his style. Referring to Jack's pauses, Johnny takes his shot, "And your takes. It's OK to be slow, but you seem to be a lazy Perry Como."

Johnny would appear on Jack's show again in October 1963, about a year after taking over *The Tonight Show*. This time, the pair's mutual respect was still intact while at the same time one begins to see that the stars' paths are crossing; Johnny on his way up to superstardom, Jack moving into the background as he gradually moves toward the comedian emeritus career stage.

Johnny would keep the cheapskate persona intact during Jack's appearances on *The Tonight Show*. In one monologue telling the audience that Jack was a guest, Johnny told a story of how Jack had the first dollar he ever earned up until that afternoon when he used it for bus fare to the studio. Jack would return the line later during the interview portion with classic Benny timing, "..that story about using my first dollar for bus fare..that's not true. The fare was $1.25." Two masters of the running gag set up and returned the comedy effectively.

The Tonight Show interviews with Jack also brought out some interesting insight into the beloved comedian. Over the years, Johnny's conversations with Jack helped us learn how much Jack truly loved the violin ("I would give up ever getting another laugh if I could have been a concert violinist."), on why it was important that he practice the violin every day ("You have to practice, even to sound lousy."), and on the shift from being Johnny's idol to Johnny becoming Jack's idol ("I can tell you now that I liked it a hell of a lot better the other way around.")

When Jack passed away in December 1974, Johnny was off from *The Tonight Show* for a few days on a planned holiday vacation. Upon his return on December 31, Johnny opened the show without a monologue. For what is believed to have been the first time since starting the show in 1962, Johnny walked out to the applause, then walked over to his desk without going center stage for the traditional monologue. My wide-eyed, teenage memory of the evening recalls Johnny making a comment along the lines of, "with that reception, maybe I shouldn't do the monologue anymore." He then began a tribute to Jack that included a long excerpt of Jack's final appearance on the Tonight Show from August 21st of that year.

A few years later, February 16, 1978, Johnny welcomed Jack's widow Mary Livingstone to his show. She had written a biography of Jack, co-written by Hilliard Marks and Marcia Borie. It was remarkable to see Mary make this appearance. She left the limelight in the 1950's due to stage fright. But in the relaxed atmosphere of Studio One at NBC's Burbank home base, she recalled the touching story about arrangements Jack had made to have a single rose delivered to her everyday following his death. The story is recounted with greater depth in the book.

Johnny used the appearance to play a portion of his college radio class presentation. Johnny asked his guests and audience to sit back and listen to an audiotape illustrating the effective use of the running gag as a comedic technique. The tape used an example from the Benny radio program.

Johnny lost his dear friend in 1974, but he never forgot that friend. He continued employing techniques learned from his long association with Jack through the end of his association with the Tonight Show. Even Johnny's departure from the show was inspired in part by Jack. He was quoted, as saying he wanted to step away from the show too soon, rather than too late. Some writers have attributed a quote to Johnny where he actually names Jack and Bob Hope as examples of stars that stayed past their prime. I have never seen tape that had that actual quote and I choose to believe that being the gentleman he was, he probably never would have actually said Jack Benny and Bob Hope stayed on TV well past their prime. Quotes attributed to Johnny in TV interviews show the king of late night simply explaining his retirement as "I'm getting out while I'm on top of my game."

Fans of Jack Benny and Johnny Carson were the beneficiaries of years of great entertainment. It was clearly a relationship based in love, respect and sincerity. These are traits that can't be faked. We saw the real thing with Jack. And we saw the real thing with Johnny. We'll probably never see something this special again.

6

Remembering Johnny

Previously unpublished. This is an appreciation of Johnny Carson. I told the story in my first book, Growing Up, Upstate about how, as a twelve-year old boy, I convinced my mom to let me stay up late on Fridays so that I could catch Johnny's show. Johnny was a big part of my young adult life. When he retired in 1992, I felt as though I was in mourning for a year.

Wow! It's been nearly twenty years since Johnny Carson left *The Tonight Show*. I remember where I was that night and how sad I felt for many weeks after.

In 1992, I was a 35-year old father of two, spending the weekend with my family at my parents' home in northern New York. My dad, who hardly ever stayed up past 9:00 PM, sat with my mom and me as we watched that final broadcast. For my parents, the end of *The Tonight Show* was merely a milestone in the raising of their son. As a junior-high student growing up, I had negotiated a deal with my folks where they'd let me stay up until 1:00 am on Friday nights so that I could watch Johnny. The rest of the week was off limits because they were school nights. I did negotiate a special Thursday night arrangement to watch *The Dean Martin Show* that ended at 11:00 pm.

Watching Johnny as a pre-teen was a real treat. Who could forget the nightly monologue, Ed, Doc, Tommy, the *Mighty Carson Art Players*, the Ed Ames tomahawk clip, Carnac, Aunt Blabby, the substitute hosts, and all those guests. To me there was no question *The Tonight Show Starring Johnny Carson* was "must see TV" in the 1970's.

I kept on making Johnny a part of my life in college and into my working life. I rarely made it to the end of his 90-minute (the format was shortened by Carson to 60-minutes nightly in 1980) broadcast, but I almost never missed the monologue and the segment immediately following the first commercial break. Fortunately, the demands of working life and raising my daughters coincided with the advent of VCR's. I was a regular time shifter, watching the previous night's broadcast the following morning, as I was getting ready for work.

When Carson announced his retirement in early 1991, I knew that his last year would be very special. Some of my friends and coworkers were already defecting to Arsenio Hall and other options available in late night programming. I knew that late night TV would change forever in less than a year when that final show would air and Johnny would leave. Johnny was basically on a yearlong farewell tour with guests lamenting his departure and the host showing his embarrassment that his retirement was creating for himself and NBC. The network was embroiled in the fallout of its highly criticized decision to have Jay Leno, and not David Letterman, replace Carson. Johnny's humble acceptance of the praise only emphasized the negatives associated with NBC bypassing its *Late Night with David Letterman* star. Carson had preferred Letterman as a successor, but was not asked to weigh in on this decision by the network bosses.

The last show was a generational milestone on par with the end of World War II and the lost innocence of the Eisenhower era following the JFK assassination. America was already changing in the early 90's, and I'd dare say life was different following May 22, 1992. Soon, we got a new President, a decade of party-driven, mean-spirited politics, and a brewing dissatisfaction with America from foreign sources.

Late night shows changed almost instantly as the new generation employed a faster pace, swooping camera shots, and worked up audiences who would gladly give standing ovations and applaud after practically every joke.

I have been told that in those closing weeks of Johnny's thirty-year NBC run, the audience regularly gave him a standing ovation. We never saw it as someone either decided it wasn't important to show the home audience how appreciative the studio audience was of Johnny, or whether Johnny himself insisted that those shots not be used.

In the years before his death, sidekick Ed McMahon published a book about his association with Johnny. *Johnny and Me*, brought tears to my eyes not so much by the actual memories of this association, but by the sense of loss Ed felt for his friend.

After all, Johnny was our friend too.

7

Andy Rooney, Writer

A column was published in the Merced Sun Star two days after Andy Rooney gave his last closing segment on 60 Minutes in October 2011. He died one month later. Here's an update to that column.

Andy Rooney gave his last regular video essay at the end of *60 Minutes* this past Sunday. He promised he would never give up the craft of writing, thanked his many fans, and apologized to anyone he may have offended by his sometimes stand offish persona.

As he stressed in his final *A Few Minutes with Andy Rooney* segment, he was and will always be a writer. That point was made clear prior to that final essay during the Morley Safer profile airing moments before Andy's swan song. Asked if he had the chance to do it all over again, Andy said he would be a writer who would read his work on *60 Minutes*. In other words, he would do the same thing again if he had the chance.

I was first exposed to his writing in junior college while taking a course in American Government. The professor played a television documentary called *Mr. Rooney Goes to Washington*. Mr. Rooney wasn't well known as a television reporter when the broadcast was produced in 1975, but he had a rich voice and he had a special style unlike many on television at the time. Of course, he wrote the documentary and did all the interviews.

The program was about wasteful spending and unyielding bureaucracy. It seems hard to believe how little time has changed.

I just found out that *Mr. Rooney Goes to Washington* received a Pulitzer Prize for excellence in television journalism that year. It clearly made the difference in Rooney's career; propelling him to the closing segment of *60 Minutes* within a couple of years and ultimately giving him the dream job he enjoyed so much for nearly a third of a century.

I copied the idea for a video project I did in that American Government class. *Mr. Newvine Goes to the Army* was about the all-volunteer military. It may still be collecting dust in the library archives at Herkimer County Community College. All I know is that I got an "A" on that project.

I watched many of Andy's closing bits throughout his tenure on *60 Minutes*. I may not have always watched the reports from Morley, Leslie, Mike, and the others. But I always tried to catch *A Few Minutes with Andy Rooney*.

It was great spending a few minutes with Andy Rooney on Sunday nights over most of my adult life. When my kids were growing up, I had to get creative as I tried to catch his closing essays at about the same time they were awarding the week's *America's Funniest Home Videos* on another channel, but I managed most times.

The comic pieces about little things were popular, but I what I appreciated most were the essays about people he knew. He chastized friend Harry Reasoner at the time of his death in 1991 for smoking cigarettes.

When he closed the July 26, 2009 edition of *60 Minutes*, Andy paid tribute to his friend Walter Chronkite who had passed away that month. I was so touched his words that I went on line to the *CBS News* website to play the tribute over and over a few times while writing down the words. It was a beautiful tribute to a friend Andy had known for nearly seventy years.

> *"I was proud to see over the years to see Walter become not only one of the best known people in television, but also one of the best known people in the world. He was proud of me too…and there is no better feeling than that. I wouldn't trade Walter Cronkite liking me for just about anything I've ever had."*

We'll miss him, and our hope that we would get to see him occasionally somewhere on television was dashed when we learned of his passing just one month after leaving *60 Minutes*.

But we still have thirty-two years of memories. And we'll always have his words.

8

Bill Cullen and Drew Carey

Previously unpublished. This is a tribute to my all time favorite game show host, Bill Cullen. It was written in 2006 just as comedian Drew Carey was about to take over hosting duties on the game show The Price is Right.

Among the program announcements on CBS television in the days prior to the start of the hosting tenure of Drew Carey was a simple no-narration spot for touting Drew as the new host of the long running *The Price is Right*.

The viewer hears the buzzer and bell sounds typical of the popular games of the 1960's and 70's. The words *The- Price- is- Right* appear on the screen, followed by a pair of dark rimmed eyeglasses and the words: "Drew Carey Hosts".

Effective? I won't second-guess the CBS promotion department brain trust. But the ad brings back to mind another glasses-wearing game show host who TV game show purists will always identify with *The Price is Right*. Bill Cullen was the original host of that game from 1956 to 1965 when that version left the airwaves. Bob Barker, who formally stepped down in June 2007, became host when the show was reformatted in 1972. The Bob Barker version and had an incredible 35 year run.

But it was Bill Cullen who helped establish the program and create a standard for TV game show hosts that continues to be followed today, more than twenty years after his death.

While best known as host for the first *The Price is Right*, he was during the 1950's, 60's and 70's, a sought out game show panelist. He was one of the four regular panelists on *I've Got a Secret* during the entire primetime run of that CBS program from 1954 through 1966. In 1969, he became a panelist on a new revamped version of *To Tell the Truth*. He stayed with that show through the late 1970's.

A quick wit and a great sense of humor best describe Bill Cullen's keys to success. Having honed his skills as a writer then announcer on Pittsburgh's KDKA radio, he made the transition to the major networks in radio and then on to television without missing a beat. His career marked many milestones in the history of television: hosting the first TV game from legendary producers Mark Goodson and Bill Todman (*Place the Face*, 1952), being among the last of most major game show hosts to leave the then traditional New York City production home base and moving his career to Los Angeles in the 1970's, and juggling as many as three game show performance assignments simultaneously (hosting *Three on a Match* and *$25,000 Pyramid* while serving as a panelist on *To Tell the Truth* in the mid-1970's).

In the early 1960's he expanded his horizons, while never abandoning his quiz hosting roots. He co-hosted holiday parades and football broadcasts. Some observers believe he was on a list of potential hosts to replace Jack Paar before Johnny Carson became the king of late night television. Retired CBS newsman Mike Wallace once told a story of how he urged Cullen to transition, as he had, into news during the mid 1960's. Cullen refused, preferring the less serious business of asking questions and giving away prizes to ordinary folks.

He was also caught up in many of the network's so-called youth movements as executives sought to open their audiences up to younger viewers. He wore leisure suits in the 1970's for one failed show (*Winning Streak*) and his trademark horned rimmed glasses were traded up for the wire framed models when they were in vogue. But even as broadcast executives talked a good game in trying to find the "young turks" to replace the more senior hosts, Bill Cullen continued to be sought after. He joked that he retired several years after he had planned because producers continued to offer him shows to host.

One such request came from producer Dan Enright of the syndicated *Joker's Wild* after the death of host Jack Berry. The 1983-84 season would be the last for *Joker's Wild* and the last regular game show series he would host. His final appearance as a panelist came in a 1987 week of shows for the newly revamped *$25,000 Pyramid* on CBS. That week of shows, the Friday episode in particular, was poignant especially when

Pyramid host Dick Clark paid homage to the "man who showed us all how to do it" during that last television appearance.

Lung cancer would take Bill Cullen from us; he passed away at the age of 70 in 1990.

Before he signed his contract to host *The Price is Right*, Drew Carey said he would do it only if Bob Barker was "cool with it". Bob was cool with it, Drew signed on. I'm sure if Bill Cullen were alive, he'd be cool with it as well. Cheers to CBS for choosing a host who will have fun with the work, will not take himself too seriously, and who will treat contestants and viewers with the respect they deserve. Just like Bill Cullen, Drew is up to the job.

9

Susanne Pleshette-TV's Enlightened Age

Previously unpublished. I'm pretty sure I'm not the only American teenage male who had a crush on Bob Newhart's TV wife from the 1970's. Here is an appreciation piece I wrote at the time of Susanne Pleshette's death.

There's been a lot of awareness in recent weeks about the so-called pioneers of television. PBS is running a series that profiles some of these performers, producers, and writers who helped blaze a trail in popular American television.

You probably won't see Suzanne Pleshette's name among those the creators of the PBS series have chosen to highlight. She should be considered among the ranks of performers who opened doors to better roles for women. She also blazed a trail so that writers could develop better characters for women, and for producers to consider women for a variety of new opportunities in the medium.

Suzanne Pleshette died in 2008 just short of her seventy-first birthday. An attractive face and deep voice got her noticed on the Broadway stage, a handful of Disney movies, and a small part in Alfred Hitchcock's *The Birds*. But the breakout role for her was playing psychologist Bob Hartley's wife Emily on *The Bob Newhart Show* in the 1970's.

It was in this classic series that she played a smart woman who respected her husband. She could dominate a scene with the deadpan Newhart without putting him down. He was never made to look like the bumbling husband and she was never marginalized to a "how was your day" transitional character whose only purpose was to show the audience the main character also had a life beyond the office.

As a young man growing up in central New York in the 1970's, Emily Hartley was a dream woman. I remember many Saturday nights when a bunch of guys would get together to watch *"Saturday Night Live"* in our Syracuse University dorm suite. I'd join in that group, but I'd also catch *The Bob Newhart Show* from earlier in the evening.

Part of the appeal of the Newhart show was Bob as a working professional. He was a psychologist and a big part of the show centered on his group therapy sessions with patients who clearly needed a lot of attention. As the first in my family to attend college, images of a professional man and woman working great jobs in a major city provided lots of motivation to get a degree.

It's easy to see how the role of Emily, coupled with the accomplishments of other 70's television icons such as Mary Tyler Moore and Carol Burnett, led to better parts written for women and better opportunities for actresses to play meaningful roles on the small screen. The Julia Louis-Dreyfus' and Tina Fey's of today's television generation owe something to the trailblazing of Suzanne Pleshette.

Though underrated in her prime, Suzanne Pleshette is now frozen in my memories of the 1970's when television moved from its' golden age to an age of enlightenment. We may choose to debate to what degree the industry may have slipped back in recent years. We'll have some wonderful memories from that 1970's age of television enlightenment. Lets remember Emily, Mrs. Robert Hartley, with a smile.

Section 3- Personal Development

I've taken a stab at sharing the advice of others as well as my thoughts on such topics as comfort zones and volunteerism. I even weigh in, with a neophyte's perspective, on what helps make a successful marriage.

10

Katie Couric and Comfort Zones

I wrote an opinion essay for the Rochester Democrat and Chronicle on Katie Couric's move to anchor the CBS Evening News in 2006. Five years later, she left the broadcast. In 2006, I used Katie's employment change to illustrate why people leave their comfort zones. My thoughts then still hold today. What follows is an updated version of that essay.

When Katie Couric took over the Managing Editor and Anchor duties at the *CBS Evening News* in 2006, I cheered.

I cheered for Katie not because she became the first woman to solo anchor a network newscast. While this is a special achievement, I really didn't think her milestone would create more than a mild blip on the list of achievements women have made in television news over the past forty years. In the 1970's when Barbara Walters became the first woman to co-anchor a network newscast, it was significant. When Connie Chung became Dan Rather's co-anchor back in the early 1990's, hardly anyone noticed.

I praised Katie's accomplishment because of the risk she took. Leaving a number one news program (*The Today Show*), a job she could probably have for the rest of her career, speaks to anyone who has taken a leap from his or her comfort zone. Trying something new at age 49 resonates with adults who see the end of their prime working years far out on the horizon, but who feel they have at least one more good shot left in them.

Over the years, I've encountered people who left their comfort zones. Most had little choice when work or family challenges forced decision-making away from the safe and secure. Others who branched out into something new did so with a strong desire to take on a challenge. I can't think of a single exception of someone in my circle of associates regretting a decision to leave their comfort zone, with or without a safety net.

Sure, Katie has a different kind of safety net than most working stiffs. But she will not wind down her working career with "what if" or "I should have taken the chance" excuses or explanations for complacency.

We now know that with the measure of ratings, Katie's move was not a success. Still, she took a chance and left her comfort zone. I still contend she still did the right thing.

11

Volunteering and a Man Named George

A newspaper clipping (Livingston News) from a successful United Way campaign. Steve is to the immediate left of the sign while George, the subject of this essay, is the first man on the right of the sign.

George's commitment to community service formed the core of an appreciation piece I wrote at the time of his death. I expanded on his volunteerism in a chapter of my book Soft Skills for Hard Times.

Volunteerism came to mind in 2008 when I had a reason to remember my friend George.

All I needed to see was his name in the subject line of an email from a mutual friend. Reading the message confirmed what I had feared: a dear friend from the past died at the age of eighty-four. With the passing of my friend George, I recalled the many lessons he taught me about community service and giving back.

I met George in 1994 when he served on the search committee that hired me as President of the local chamber of commerce. He was the toughest questioner on the panel, taking exception for not having adequate community service on my resume. I offered explanations about how my work in local television news didn't afford time for much community service.

He didn't care for that response and he let me know it. He was right. Fortunately for me, George and the search committee saw some potential and recommended that I be hired.

Throughout my ten years as President of the chamber, George was our resident historian, a great sounding board for ideas, and a trusted friend. He knew he could always stop by my office to discuss issues impacting business in the community. He had a sixth sense that seemed to tell him I needed to talk. Interestingly, his visits usually came following one of his many volunteer meetings for at a number of community organizations

When the chamber's ambitious program of work seemed next to impossible to handle, George gave me a piece of advice in the form of a Latin phrase. The phrase, translated, is "little by little, you can achieve a lot". Again, his advice was right on target. I have found his method of breaking down large projects into smaller, more manageable tasks, to be one of the secrets of my success in these later years of my professional career.

I found out that George got that bit of advice from his beloved wife Beth. She is a dedicated volunteer as well. She knows a lot about keeping organized and George frequently thanked her publicly for her contributions to their successful marriage and their many volunteer activities.

I last spoke to George in late 2006 to discuss an issue facing the board of a non-profit I was serving on in California. He was flattered that I would call him. I was honored that he'd take the time to talk. His humility was there; he never mentioned that the local chamber of commerce had just named a community service award in his honor.

So many organizations owed their existence to George's diligence. His persistence and willingness to do the heavy lifting was directly responsible for a number of organizations that continue to thrive in the community. Organizations suddenly got scores of volunteers for a one-time project thanks to his "working the phones" to round up help. All of this was done without fanfare. And there are the countless acts of kindness, the ones that get no headlines or pats on the back. For example, some people were offered rides to a doctor's appointment. Volunteer judges for a local oratory competition suddenly appeared once the word went out from George that their help was needed. Deceased veterans were presented with full military honors thanks to his (and other veterans) insistence that no person who served our nation on the battlefield should be laid to rest without this ceremony.

When George died, his community lost a true disciple of the ideals behind giving back.

The communities of Caledonia and Mumford in Western New York, published a tribute to George on the website Caledonia-Mumford.com that enumerated many acts of kindness. It opens with a simple premise suggesting that if there ever were a book written about George, the common theme would be community service leadership.

> "It would contain page after page of accounts of ... (George)... seeing a need in the life of someone less fortunate or envisioning a way to make their world a little bit better and doing something about it. Throughout the chapters, only the names of the people whose lives he helped improve would change."

He was a generous man, a passionate defender of our freedoms, and a true friend.

Little by little, he accomplished so much.

12

The Commencement Speech

This essay has an interesting history. The passage dealing with my personal affirmation- I am a prize, was published in my book Soft Skills for Hard Times. A version with the commencement speech angle appeared in the Merced Sun Star. It was inspired by a moment in my professional life where I was on the verge of losing my confidence.

I've never been asked to give a commencement speech. But I have heard enough of them over the years to make me think I'm an expert.

For the graduating class of 2010, a professional life is just beginning to develop. The commencement speech is the start to that career. It can be the equivalent of a coach's locker room pep talk before the graduate goes out to face life as a working person.

The speech will most likely be forgotten. I urge this year's graduating seniors to listen to the speech anyway. Savor the words, accept the diploma, and go out in the real world to pursue your passion.

The commencement speech I never gave would center on just a few points about being successful at work and in life. I would talk about the soft skills. I would urge the graduates to treat everyone as a customer. I'd remind them to show up for work on time and have a good attitude on the job.

I'd encourage them to volunteer at something, consider a spiritual existence, and respect your family.

I would tell the class of 2010 to write thank-you notes, and to write these notes with a pen and not a computer. I'd tell them to always look for ways to continue their education throughout their lives and become lifelong learners.

And I would share with them a story about myself that I call "I am a prize."

"I am a prize" is an attitude shift I adopted after experiencing a rejection following a job interview several years ago.

At the time, I felt I had more than my share of rejections. I wondered whether some friends had suddenly abandoned me. I began wallowing in self-doubt as to whether I could actually ever experience success at the workplace ever again.

The specific instance when I felt I had been pushed too far on the negative side of the job search pendulum isn't important anymore. But I do recall at the time, after leaving a job interview and "reviewing" the interview in my head on the drive back home, I reached an epiphany.

"If these people pass on me, they are missing out on the best person for the job," I told myself as I drove down the highway. "It will be their loss, for I am a prize!"

These were comforting words to help me get over a negative job interview experience.

But they were also empowering words.

The words set about an attitude adjustment. I experienced a mindset shift from feeling powerless to feeling empowered. It set up a positive energy flow. From that moment on, I was renewed with energy that helped me find a new opportunity that opened a whole new world of opportunities.

"I am a prize."

As the negative experience moved from my psyche, it was replaced with the realization that I am worthwhile.

I remember feeling that I was worthy of honorable work, that I did bring value to my family and friends, and that there was no reason to expect any less from myself if given the chance to contribute at the workplace.

"Not everyone will see this," I thought to myself, "But someone will."

"I am a prize."

And so, I would tell the class of 2010 that they too must tell themselves every day that they are worthwhile, they are worthy of honorable work, and that they bring value to their relationships.

I would tell them to look at themselves in the mirror every morning and tell themselves, "I am a prize."

As individuals, we have so much to give others and so much to give ourselves. I encourage every member of the class of 2010 to affirm that belief in their heart and show it with confidence and enthusiasm.

Experiences define you. Life's ups and downs have polished your persona.

You are a prize!

Enjoy life. Enjoy the journey.

Steve & Vaune Newvine (Newvine personal collection)

13

Marriage

Previously unpublished

When it comes to marriage, I wonder who is an expert? Certainly not me.

I've been at it for thirty-two years and I'm still learning something new every day about being married.

Once Vaune and I reached the twenty-five year mark, I began making a point to seek out the so-called secrets of a successful marriage. At first, I'd listen to famous people explain how their marriages lasted so long.

Actor and director Carl Reiner answered Johnny Carson's question about the secret to a successful union with the response, "The key is marry someone who can stand you."

The wife of actor Samuel L. Jackson gave a CBS Sunday Morning reporter a one-word answer to the same question. Her response to what makes a successful marriage: amnesia.

One morning while away from home during a business trip, I heard the newly married local television news anchor woman give her advice to a man who recently announced his engagement: "All I can say is that if she cooks dinner and you think it's good, tell her it's great!"

Radio talk show host Sean Hannity told a listener once that if your focus is always on making the other person happy, then you'll never have any worries in marriage.

I don't know where I heard this next piece of advice, but it makes a lot of sense to me: "never go to bed angry...you won't get to sleep anyway."

At church one Sunday, the priest offered a special prayer to a couple celebrating their seventieth anniversary. After the service, I asked the husband what was the secret to a long marriage. Without missing a beat, this ninety-year old man looked at me and said, "Learn how to say yes dear."

I look around and see many blessings of long marriages in my family. My parents celebrated forty-eight years with my dad taking care of my mom as she fought her losing battle with cancer. On the night before she passed away, he knelt down close to the head of the bed and said her prayers for her. Actions certainly spoke louder than words that night.

My grandparents on my dad's side of the family made it to their seventy-second anniversary. I'm not sure what either one would say was their secret to a long last union. But I remember hearing stories about how willing my Grandpa was to help Grandma with the household chores when my dad was growing up. I thought that was unusual when I heard the story as a child. I had a different perspective once I had children of my own.

Maybe that's the secret to a successful marriage. It may not be the spoken word or the written pieces of advice. Love is often in the unspoken. Love is knowing that the other person needs you to step up, and tend to the business at hand.

A priest once told couples preparing for the Catholic sacrament of matrimony that marriage was not a fifty-fifty proposition: with both partners agreeing to compromise. Rather, this man's contention was that marriage was one hundred percent give from both partners. I'll go with that. One hundred percent seems like a good place to start.

14

The Apology

This is an edited version of an opinion essay I wrote for the Merced Sun Star in 2010.

There was a lot of attention paid to the ten-minute apology speech given by Tiger Woods on February 19, 2010. News and sports analysts spent most of the days leading up to the speech anticipating what Tiger would say and speculating whether it would be sincere enough to get him past the scandals surrounding his infidelities. These same analysts are being called upon now to weigh in on the apology.

The pundits have a lot to work with: Was the apology sincere enough? Is Tiger truly sorry? When will he play golf again?

At least one good thing has come from Tiger's time in front of a selected group of family, friends, and sports writers on that Friday morning. The act of taking responsibility for one's actions may focus some attention on the apology as a soft skill in the workplace and in life.

Everyone makes mistakes; and every supervisor and employee has made a mistake at work. Not everyone who has made a mistake at work will apologize. That's a big problem with the world of work today.

Whether it's the mid-level supervisor who blankets an entire work team with a mistaken email chastisement on a project, a senior manager who pushes a cost cutting initiative to the point of causing irreparable productivity losses, or an entry level employee who wastes time checking on personal business during office hours, workers make mistakes. But how often do these workers take the time to apologize? Most of the time, if an apology is offered, it comes only after the infraction has been discovered. Often, that may be too little, too late.

There are exceptions that produce positive results. In a book I wrote about soft skills at work, I detail a story heard on a Public Television special about a mid-level supervisor who was forced by his boss to apologize to a subordinate. Reluctantly, the supervisor offered the apology. When word of the apology spread throughout the work team, efficiency improvements happened at the job site almost immediately. The apology was not only the right thing to do; it also resulted in improved customer service as the staff rose to the occasion of a supervisor taking responsibility for a mistake.

There are some lessons we can take from Tiger's apology. Watching it unfold, it appeared to touch on the three points of an appropriate statement of contrition: sincerity, no qualification such as the "if I offended anyone, then I'm sorry" line, and an action plan to assure those offended that the behavior will not happen again. There was a moment where he began to point the finger at the media for hounding his family. But taken as a whole, this "apology event" was a significant step in the rehabilitation journey.

As teachable moments go, we can all take something from the events surrounding Tiger's apology. People expect apologies. We react well to sincerity. We don't like it when the person making amends is pointing the finger at something else. And we appreciate knowing that there's more to the process than just standing up at the podium and speaking up.

We all hope Tiger Woods rises from this low point and rebuilds the trust he lost as a result of his indiscretions. Let's hope everyone watching or reading his story can glean a few lessons about the value of a sincere apology.

Section 4-Moon Rocks

The American Space program captured my imagination at a very early age. It has never really left me, even though I often feel as though it has left the minds and hearts of some of our national government leaders.

Steve with a moon rock at the Challenger Learning Center in Atwater, California
(Photo from Steve's personal collection)

15

Moon Rocks- A Fascination with Space

From MercedCountyEvents.com

The picture seems just right for a guy who fell in love with the space program as a kid growing up in the 1960's. Taken by Joseph Minafra of Lockheed Martin, there's a smiling yours truly holding a moon rock picked up by one of the astronauts during Apollo 16. Joseph and another colleague from Lockheed were in Atwater on June 10, 2011 for the twentieth anniversary celebration of the Challenger Learning Center on the grounds of the former Castle Air Force Base.

Growing up during the formative years of America's race to the moon, I remember most of the rocket launches. The three major networks televised all American manned rocket launches in those pre-cable saturation days. Whether you liked it or not, a NASA launch was the only thing on.

But I liked it. I was amazed by the firepower of those rockets. I took in with great interest the grainy video of John Glenn and his fellow astronauts. The Mercury program started things for US manned space flight. Gemini followed, and it would lead into the Apollo program. It seemed as though I watched every launch.

The television anchormen and reporters who covered the launches were filled with the sense of excitement that this was a really special, truly American, accomplishment. Back in the 1960's, no other country, save for the Soviet Union, was even coming close to achieving what the United States was accomplishing with the space program.

The enthusiasm endured even as the nation continued to get mired down in the tragedy of Vietnam. But a setback in 1967 would but the brakes on the program at least for a little while.

I was away with my dad and brother at a winter camp the night we heard on the radio that Apollo 1 had experienced a fire that killed three astronauts during a systems test. I was nine years old and like many Americans, I felt that our race to the moon might be stalled for the rest of the decade.

But the Apollo program returned, and soon our focus was back on the moon and doing that in a safer manner. I remember the Life magazine cover of Apollo 8 going around the moon and sending back a picture of the big blue and white marble that was Earth at Christmas time in 1968. I started a scrapbook as the nation, and the world, anxiously awaited the launch of Apollo 11. Two more missions would push the envelope even further as the world waited for the big one.

The astronaut team of Neil Armstrong, Buzz Aldrin, and Ed Collins were our heroes as that "small step for man… giant leap for mankind" took place in July 1969. Their mission was a success. They brought back the incredible story of an unimaginable adventure.

And they brought back moon rocks.

Over the next few years, five more missions (Apollo 13 did not land on the moon) to the lunar surface would create more fascinating stories, and more rocks. There's a scene in the movie *Apollo 13* where the stranded astronauts momentarily question why their spacecraft calculations seem to be off by a few hundred pounds. Two astronauts look at each other with one saying, "Rocks." The calculations were based on a returning spacecraft that would have included lunar samples.

I guess that's why the moon rock on display at the Challenger Learning Center really hit home for me. Here was a piece of the moon, encased in Lucite, a specimen from our great adventure into space. I could hold it, and smile with it as the picture was taken. It completes the scrapbook I started as a kid.

Over the years, I met several astronauts in my travels as a space reporter in Huntsville, Alabama in the early 1980's including Wally Schirra from the original Mercury Seven. In the 1990's, I met Jim Lovell and Fred Haise, the two surviving members of the famous Apollo 13 mission that had to return from space after an explosion nearly lost the spacecraft. The pair was reunited at a conference I attended in upstate

New York. Meeting these modern day explorers was nothing short of a dream come true for this boy who loved the space program.

But seeing the moon rock, something that actually came back from America's journey into the unknown, was a very special moment in my life.

Ever since Apollo ended, there has been debate over why the United States ended manned lunar exploration. As the space shuttle program ended in 2011, the discussion continues over why our nation is backing away from manned space flight.

For this one special night in Atwater, California, there was no debate. There was no discussion over our space budget priorities. For this one night, this little boy who grew up never losing faith in American ingenuity, the moon rock brought it all home.

16

Apollo 11- Where Were You

This was published in the Merced Sun Star in 2009 to mark the fortieth anniversary of Apollo 11, the first moon landing.

Where were you the night Neil Armstrong and Buzz Aldrin walked on the moon?

That special night forty years ago this week will be easy for many of us to remember. The moon landing had a great build-up in the media. The nation was behind the Apollo 11 team as the astronauts met with reporters, detailed their daily moves, and brought home the pictures of what could be described as one of mankind's greatest accomplishments.

I was a twelve-year-old boy who followed the developments leading up to the mission carefully. I had a scrapbook of newspaper clippings, a model of the Saturn Five rocket with breakaway pieces of the Apollo capsule and the lunar landing module, and lots of enthusiasm for this moment in history about to be showcased on the television in my family living room.

When the day finally arrived, I spent most of it enjoying the rides, games and food associated with the Port Leyden Firemen's Field Days in upstate New York. My family left the carnival early so that we wouldn't miss a moment of the moon landing.

My memory is still fairly clear about that night. I recall it seemed to me then that it took Armstrong an awful long time to place that first step on the moon surface. The video was grainy and in black and white.

But when the moment finally came, the significance of the event became perfectly clear.

"It's one small step for man, one giant leap for mankind."

Years of hard work were summed up with those eleven words. Hundreds of space agency employees and thousands of contract workers saw their efforts rewarded. Three astronauts lost their lives in that horrible fire on the launch pad just a few years before. All of us were united as we saw NASA carry out the mission set by President Kennedy at the start of the decade.

"This nation should commit itself to achieving the goal, before this decade is out, of landing a man on the Moon and returning him safely to the Earth."

Over the years, I have continued my fascination over space. The Apollo 13 mission captured everyone's attention thanks to the Tom Hanks movie. I remember listening to news updates, but not being terribly concerned as to how dangerous that mission really was at the time. In the early 1980's, I was a TV reporter in Huntsville, Alabama covering the Marshall Space Flight Center when the Space Shuttle Columbia ushered in a new era of space travel. And I'll never forget staring in disbelief from a newsroom in Rochester, New York when the networks cut into regular programming to announce that the Challenger had exploded. My colleagues absorbed the news, and then moved quickly to prepare our local coverage of the tragedy.

I've been blessed to have met about a half-dozen astronauts in my professional life: John Young and Robert Crippen from the first shuttle mission, Joe Engle and Richard Truly from the second shuttle mission, along with Walter Schirra, Fred Haise, and Jim Lovell from the Apollo program.

I've always remarked that for men who seemed larger than life, most were of slight build. They probably had to be in order to fit into the small space capsules. This has been a reminder that strength and courage have little to do with physical ability and size.

America's space program has been as much a part of my life as growing up in a small town and using my imagination to envision a lifetime of experiences. I celebrated its' accomplishments, I mourned its' tragedies, and I learned a little more about myself with each mission. The past forty years saw me transition from a child to a teen, from an elementary school student straight through high school to a college graduate, from a husband to a father, and from a wide-eyed dreamer to a seasoned veteran of life. I'd like to think that the optimism I've experienced along this journey was inspired in some way by those men who took President Kennedy up on his challenge and made the moon landing possible.

And I'd like to think that keeping my own momentum going throughout these past forty years has been due, in some part, to the continued dedication of the men and women who have dreamed the dreams that have formed the basis for our many discoveries in space and science.

This anniversary is for all of us.

Steve and Photographer Jim Hatchett at the Marshall Space Flight Center, Huntsville, Alabama in 1982   (Steve Newvine Personal Collection)

17

The End of the Shuttle Program

Previously unpublished

In an earlier career as a television journalist, I covered the Space Shuttle, NASA's new space program, thirty years ago. I was a beat reporter working at WAAY-TV in Huntsville, Alabama. Huntsville was the home of the Marshall Space Flight Center, the NASA facility charged with managing the development of the shuttle's engines and solid rocket boosters. Space was an important beat for a young reporter. The station's News Director Mike Sullivan thought I'd be ideal for that role and I liked the idea of making new contacts within Marshall and producing stories.

I was charged with developing feature reports on projects underway at NASA and how the Marshall Space Flight Center interfaced with these projects. Week after week, I'd turn in stories on some of the fascinating projects being worked on at the space agency. NASA always seemed to have some pretty good animation video they would provide to help illustrate the project. Media managers at Marshall were always willing to provide a spokesperson to be interviewed on camera.

A lot of our stories centered on the shuttle program. After years of delays, NASA said it was ready to launch the first Space Transportations System (or STS-1 in NASA's language). My station had big plans to cover the local connection to this national story. We would have our relatively new "live-eye" microwave transmitting van at the Marshall

Center so that I could broadcast from Marshall before and after the network coverage of the launch.

There was a launch date planned in early 1981, so we made our plans and got ready for the big story. Our team that morning included our anchorman, a producer, our news director, a camera operator, and our live-eye technician. We met for a pre-launch breakfast production meeting at a local IHOP. As it turned out, our local coverage really served as a run-through for the real thing. Shortly after arriving at Marshall, we learned that a computer glitch would delay the launch. About an hour later, we learned that the launch would be postponed.

The launch was rescheduled for April 12, 1981. This time, we didn't have a pre launch breakfast. Our coverage did our community proud. The Marshall team played a critical role in the success of the program, and our television station had the local story covered from every conceivable angle.

That mission would last two days and went off without any problems. It landed at Edwards Air Force Base in Kern and San Bernardino Counties here in California. Shuttles would eventually land at the Kennedy Space Center with Edwards serving as a back up landing site.

Several weeks later, astronauts John Young and Robert Crippen visited the Marshall Space Flight Center to thank the workers who helped make the mission a success. Again, I covered the local story for the Huntsville TV station. I interviewed both men. The picture accompanying this essay shows me narrating over a camera shot of the plane carrying Young and Crippen.

I would cover the next two shuttle launches including *STS 3* that lifted off the day after my first daughter Alison was born in 1982. I covered the morning launch, recorded an audio track of my report, and headed off to the hospital to be with my wife and my new baby.

We left Huntsville for a new opportunity at a station in the Midwest after *STS 4* later in the summer.

A few years later, I had moved from that station in the Midwest to a station in Rochester, New York. I was in the newsroom that cold January 28, 1986 morning when the shuttle *Discovery* exploded after lift-off. I stood in the center of the newsroom in stunned silence. After watching the first twenty-minutes of *ABC News* coverage, I realized we had work to do. I helped reshape our newscast for our six o'clock broadcast. Gone were all the stories planned for the day. Each team of reporters and photographers were reassigned the local angle of this national tragedy. We had a crew at an electronics store where every television set on display had the images of the shuttle. Another crew was in a classroom to talk to teachers and students about the tragedy (this was the mission with teacher Christa McAulliffe as part of the crew).

As we were putting these stories together for that night's newscast, I made a news judgment decision that wasn't well received by many of my colleagues. After watching the replay over and over throughout the afternoon, I decided that our viewers would not be subjected to that horrible video more than once during our six PM newscast. Video editors complained that they wouldn't have sufficient footage to cover the reporters' narration. Reporters argued that the explosion was the story and therefore, fair game. I held firm; and thanks to the back up by my boss, a News Director by the name of Gil Buettner, the rule stayed in effect throughout the newscast.

Our program began with the pictures of the countdown, and then our anchor team faced the camera to acknowledge that most of our viewers had probably already seen the tragedy and that we would show it only one more time. After that announcement, we ran a short video of the actual explosion.

That decision to spare our audience another half-hour of shuttle explosion replays remains the one I am most proud of during my fifteen years in the television news business.

Covering the space program for that brief period thirty years ago was a very special time for me. It was a uniquely American story. I left television news as I embarked on new career paths that would eventually take my wife and me to the Central Valley.

While I wouldn't trade anything that I do now for the career I had in the electronic news media, I still look back on those years covering the space program as a local television reporter with considerable pride.

We will say our goodbyes to a thirty-year mission that attempted to make space flight seem almost ordinary, but there is nothing routine about sending men and women into space. They, and the thousands of workers on the ground who played a role in building the space program are truly courageous and dedicated individuals. We owe them our respect and gratitude.

Section 5- Growing up in the 60's and 70's

It seems my bread and butter in writing columns centers on my experiences as a youth in Port Leyden, New York. I had a childhood that is probably considered ordinary. But I continue to think of people, events, and places from that special time as it helps me paint a clearer picture of what life was like back in the 1960's and 70's.

18

Reflections on 1968

This is an updated version of a column that first appeared in the Merced Sun Star in 2008.

So much has been written this year about 1968. There have been examinations of the year in terms of the cultural shift it represented in Tom Brokaw's book *Boom*. We've seen forty-year anniversary pieces in all the news magazines that include retrospectives of the death of Martin Luther King. Soon, we will read similar anniversary essays on the life and death of Robert Kennedy.

My recollections from that very formative year in my life center around what was going on in my world back then. In 1968, I was an eleven-year old boy growing up in a small upstate New York village where all my relatives lived within an hour of my home. We were a close-knit family, as most families were forty years ago.

My perspective forty years later, centers on my broader world view based on living three-thousand miles from my boyhood home, far away from the friends and family I knew so well so long ago. Thanks to phone calls and email, I cope with an internal struggle to keep close to my friends and family back east.

As a fifth grader at Port Leyden Elementary School, my first lasting memory of 1968 was the principal's office where I was spending my lunchtime for a week in March of that year. My teacher, Mrs. James, sent me there as punishment following some long-forgotten fight with another fifth grader. The principal thought a week of quiet time during the lunch recess might teach us both a lesson. I remember my birthday falling into that week, and how I missed the traditional singing of *Happy Birthday* in the lunchroom. I also remember the other student given the same disciplinary action was absent the entire week.

Somehow, the innocence of being sent to the principal's office was erased as the month of April moved in. Within days, the news of the shooting death of Dr. King suddenly brought the topic of racism and the struggle for civil rights into the classroom. In 1968 upstate New York, there wasn't a person of color within a fifty-mile radius of Port Leyden. Dr. King's death, and the extensive television coverage that was shown in every classroom, brought about a greater awareness in my fifth grade class that there was an ugly issue still percolating in our nation. The subject of race was now being talked about nationally and the civil rights movement was a topic of discussion in my fifth grade classroom.

April passed into May with personal tragedy. My uncle Billy was killed in an automobile accident in early May, about one-month to the day of Dr. King's death. Billy was just twenty-three years old, home from his eighteen-month tour of duty in Vietnam, and just beginning his post military service life when his car went off the highway late one Saturday night. I was away on a Boy Scout camping trip that weekend. I learned about the accident upon my return home on Sunday. The parent who drove my fellow scouts and I back from the camping trip remained quiet along the ride home knowing that I would receive the bad news from my parents soon enough. At age eleven, I had encountered death in the family before. But never so ironically as I dealt with the sad fact that this veteran of our nation's war in Vietnam, returning to start his postwar life, had that life taken away so tragically. I had never experienced such visible signs of grief than the tears and lost looks I saw on the faces of my grandparents.

Tragedy struck again in early June when Robert Kennedy was killed in Los Angeles. Again, the black and white television set in my fifth grade classroom was filled with the story of the nation grieving. The adults in my life would use phrases such as "what is this world coming to" and "I wonder who is next". With memories of the JFK assassination from four-and-a-half years earlier still in my mind, I began to have those same feelings as the adults. *What was this world coming to?*

Somehow, I made it through fifth grade. The summer of 1968 would bring the Democratic Convention and the scenes of riots in the streets of Chicago. By now, I was hardened to the images of violence. I really appreciated my small town with old-fashion values and no crime.

I entered sixth grade that fall and watched the presidential campaign race to the finish with Richard Nixon's promise to end the Vietnam war appear to be more convincing to voters than Hubert Humphrey's promise to end the Vietnam war.

My grandparents' grief over the loss of their youngest son would move through the various stages. Eventually, the pain wasn't so obvious to us, but we knew it was there.

My life growing up in upstate New York was filled with great memories and heart-tugging experiences. I would not have traded it for anything. 1968 was the beginning of a transition for me from childhood innocence to adolescent awareness of the world around me.

Forty-three years later, I realize that even with the tragedies of that year, making it through the difficult times in 1968 helped me grow and prepared me for the rest of my adult life.

19

Marking the End of the Pontiac

I have my dad, Ed Newvine, to thank for this update of a piece that first appeared in the Merced Sun Star in 2009. When I sent him the clipping from the newspaper, he told me he liked the article, but the family car I was writing about was actually a Pontiac Star Chief, not a Bonneville as I had originally written.

The federal government's plan to restructure General Motors is designed to improve the finances for the ailing automaker. The plan also calls for the end of production for the Pontiac line. While the car guys (and women) are mourning the end of Pontiac, I'll miss that familiar brand for reasons that have little to do with muscle cars such as the Firebird or the GTO.

For my family growing up in Port Leyden, New York during the 1960's and 70's, Pontiac was the family car. In the mid-sixties, my dad brought home a used 1964 Pontiac Star Chief. From that moment onward until after I left home to enter the workforce, Pontiacs were part of our household.

I remember that Star Chief. It was mauve with a white top. Headlights were two to a side and stacked vertically. It had four doors and lots of legroom no matter where you sat. It also had, arguably, the largest trunk in the history of auto making. The cars were big, reliable, powerful, and apparently cheap to run (although no one thought much about the price of gas in these days that preceded the Middle East oil embargo of the early 1970's).

I have no idea how big the engine was. All I remember is the Star Chief was able to tow our family camper trailer during our summer outings to the Adirondack Mountains. The large trunk came in handy, as our family of five would fill it with suitcases for our annual winter trip to visit my grandparents in Florida. That adventure was three thousand miles round-trip, and the Bonneville got us there and back every year.

Over the years, Dad would replace these late model used Pontiacs with other Pontiacs. He bought a brand new Catalina in 1972. Not much had changed: four door, big trunk, and all the amenities of its' predecessors with one new feature: new car smell.

Pontiac was the only car in our driveway when we were a one-car family. When we became a two-car family as my brother and I got our drivers' licenses, we became a two-Pontiac family.

I'll never forget the night I had the family car out past my curfew. Dad was upset and like most fathers in that era, he let me know it with a good tongue-lashing. I'll never forget his lament, "It's not like gas is cheap anymore. Why it's fifty-cents a gallon!" What we would give for those days.

As a young family man looking to replace my Toyota pick up truck, I tried to buy a Pontiac in the 1980's. I even went as far as to drive into a Pontiac dealership. But once the salesman determined what my price range was, he directed me to a lower-priced used Plymouth Reliant.

I'll mark the passing of the Pontiac line with a little more heartfelt poignancy than I did with the end of such lines as Plymouth Reliant, Oldsmobile, and (thankfully) the AMC Pacer. The car guys may miss their GTO's, Firebirds, and Grand Ams. But I'll miss my Dad's Star Chief, and all the memories created with it growing up.

20

The Edison

Edison phonograph (Photo: Newvine personal collection)

Inspired by a passage in my book Growing Up, Upstate, this is the full essay from Merced County Events.com

My Grandma Newvine had an *Edison* phonograph in her home. As an elementary school aged grandson, I would always look forward to her cranking up the machine and playing the half-inch thick records. As I moved into my middle and high school years, she'd let me go into the back room of her house and play the records by myself.

I loved spending an afternoon cranking up the *Edison* with the arm on the side of the cabinet. I'd pull out a record from the cabinet, set it on the turntable, and start up the music. The scratches and skips on the records were part of the character of the experience. I truly enjoyed the collection of waltzes, fox trots, sopranos, tenors, and lullabies

The music was nice, but I really liked the comedy routines. Among the vaudeville era bits was a little ditty my grandmother called *The Recipe*.

The comedian, unknown as the record label has been long lost, begins with a recipe for a casserole. After commenting on the various ingredients and directions, the performer ends the recipe with the instructions, "throw it out and open a can of salmon". He then sings about a woman named Ann:

> *Talk about Ann,*
> *In her little sedan.*
> *Who did we up in the tree-zies,*
> *Hanging by their X-Y Zee-zies.*
> *Ann,*
> *In her little sedan.*

I was the only grandchild who had any real interest in Grandma's record player. When she was in her ninety's, she gave the phonograph to me. She passed away a few years later. Before she died, I produced a ten-minute holiday video with my two daughters singing Christmas carols accompanied by a xylophone recording on the *Edison*. Grandma got to see how I intended to keep the tradition of the antique phonograph alive for future generations.

The antique phonograph was a great conversation starter for visitors to our home. It made several moves as we traded up to different homes over the years.

One of those moves resulted in something apparently getting loose within the phonograph cabinet. The *Edison* would no longer play. We promised ourselves to get it fixed one of these days, but that day never came. It sat in the corner of our living room: still a conversation starter, but no longer a source of entertainment.

Then one summer night, we had several people over to our house for a party. Naturally, the *Edison* again started a conversation. As I explained how the phonograph stopped playing in recent years, my wife demonstrated how the crank arm worked. She turned on the turntable, and the record started spinning.

We played several records for our guests that evening. One of them commented to us in a thank you note: "So nice when what was old becomes new again".

I don't know why the *Edison* started working again. But I do believe in small gifts of fate. And this was one of those gifts.

21

Joe Dunn and the Dry Goods Store

The welcome sign to Port Leyden, New York. (Steve Newvine personal collection)

Growing Up, Upstate proved to me that I could write a book, that people would read it, and that I could embrace a lot of memories. Here is a section on a storeowner from Main Street, Port Leyden, New York. I'm planning a second book on Port Leyden in late 2012.

Joe Dunn ran a dry goods store in Port Leyden. By the time I got to know him, he was getting ready to close the store and retire. His store had a comic book rack, so I found myself going in there frequently to check out the latest issues of Batman and Archie comics.

The comic book rack was actually a full blown magazine rack, with the comics on the lower shelves, teen magazines at eye level, and adult magazines such as the ones about motorcycles, fishing, and race cars above that. At the very top, well outside the reach of a curious fourth-grader, were the men's magazines. In these pre-brown paper wrapper days, about all I could see from my vantage point was the magazine title along that top shelf. Occasionally, a man would grab an issue from that very top rack, and thumb through it while I was scanning *Batman* and *Superman*. But I didn't get to see much in those early days.

I was a little chubby in the mid sixties so Joe nicknamed me Slim. It didn't bother me. I enjoyed his company. His store sold shoes, construction clothes, farmer overalls, winter jackets, hunting hats, sweatshirts, jack knives, and hundreds of other items. Back in the forties and fifties, it probably did a swift business. By the sixties, more retailers had entered the marketplace and trips to nearby Utica where the discount stores were popping up, began to take business away from these traditional dry goods stores.

Joe was at retirement age anyway and apparently had invested well over the years. He went out of business in 1968 and died the next year. I still have a stack of comic books I bought from his store when I was a kid. I checked the value on E-bay, but only for curiosity sake. I'd never sell them. The memories associated with Joe and his store are more meaningful to me.

Joe made a difference to me because he was the first non-relative adult to treat me as a friend.

22

My Eight Years as an Altar Boy

Edited from MercedCountyEvents.com

I got to thinking recently about some of the times I experienced as a boy and young adult in upstate New York. In particular, I recall the years I was an Altar Boy at St. Martin's Church in Port Leyden.

I started when I was in the fourth grade. Sister Mary Agnes was our trainer. We practiced weekly after school at the church. Our practice began with a prayer, then repetition of the elements of the Catholic Mass.

We learned when to genuflect, how to genuflect, how to hold the book of priest prayers, when to get the water and wine, how to hold the gold-plated paten under the chin of persons receiving Holy Communion, and when to ring the bells during the Eucharistic Prayers.

Week after week, we'd go to practice. Week after week, we'd review each segment of the celebration while learning what to do and what not to do. But week after week, Sister told us we were still not ready.

Eventually, we would each be issued a black cassock and a while surplice. This was the official "uniform" of a server. We were told to take the cassock and surplice home and "have our Mom wash and iron them". It was another step toward getting an assignment.

Finally, I got the call. One afternoon after school, Sister phoned my home to tell me that I would have my first assignment on the altar. I was told I would be "serving on the side", which meant that I wouldn't have to actually do any of the things I had been taught during the past five months. My only job was to show up with my cassock and surplice, process out of the priest's sanctuary with the other "real" servers at the beginning of Mass, and sit on the side of the altar throughout the service.

I was nervous and recall being pushed out onto the altar from one of the senior servers when my feet appeared to be stuck to the floor at the start of the Mass. But I got through it. I think my Dad was in the congregation that first night. My Mom had not yet converted to Catholicism.

Within weeks, I would get my shot at actually serving as a "real" server. By the next year, I fancied myself one of the senior types who helped the newbies overcome their nervousness.

Over the years, I was tempted to give up my altar serving. Several of the boys who started with me that first year had already dropped out of the ministry. Some were not even coming to church anymore. The temptation to end my stint as an altar boy was strong. After all I reasoned, *I was a teenager and the cassock and surplice were not really cool.* But with some encouragement from my Dad to stick with it, I persevered. By the time I was a senior in high school, serving on the altar was a badge of honor I wore proudly.

The last Mass I served at St. Martin's was the day after my high school graduation. I still wonder if Sister Agnes Claire purposely scheduled me for that day so that I wouldn't be tempted to overdo it on the partying after the graduation ceremony. I'll never know.

Our priest during those late teen years was Father Lyddy: a kind man and a good teacher. As we continued to grow into our roles, Father Lyddy allowed my friend Phil and me to read scripture as a Lector during Masses when we were serving. That is where I got my first opportunity to Lector. Little by little, he was introducing us to other ministries in the Church

Serving on the altar also cemented my friendship with Phil. The two of us had known each other since kindergarten, but our time as Altar Boys at St. Martin's created a unique bond that remains to this day.

I'll always remember Holy Week when I was in my late teens. For an Altar Boy, this was the World Series of serving with three special celebrations followed by the Easter Sunday Mass. There were special rehearsals for these services. By then, Phil and I were always assigned the Mass on Holy Thursday, the service on Good Friday, and the Easter Vigil Mass on Holy Saturday.

Many times after Holy Thursday and Holy Saturday services, Phil and I would just stand outside the church and talk for what seemed to a good hour or more. While we both remained friends, both of us had expanded our base of friends to include others. But our service together as Altar Servers created a special bond.

I'm grateful for those eight years as an Altar Boy. I'm certain it kept me engaged in a church going culture that existed in my family during my years growing up. My service built a foundation for my volunteer work in church ministry that continues to this day. But most of all, I associate my time as an Altar Boy as a positive experience that I wouldn't have traded for anything. It was indeed a blessing.

Section 6-Passings

I have delivered eulogies for three family members, and I have written at least a half dozen columns that center on the death of someone. Whether it was a noted author, a friend, or a person who touched my life in some way I have used words to deal with grief by writing or speaking about a person who has made an impact on my life.

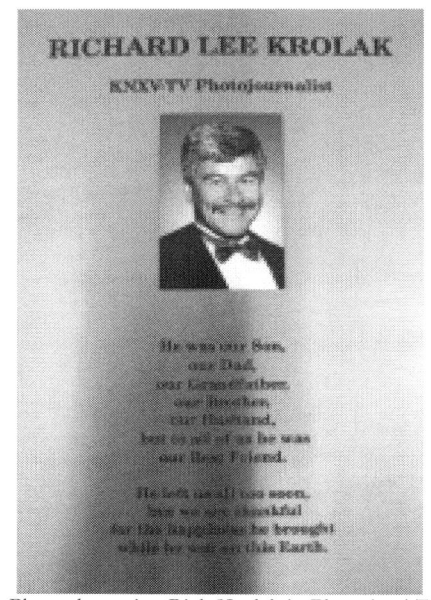

- Plaque honoring Rick Korlak in Phoenix, AZ
(Plaque photo from RickKrolak.com)

23

Rick Krolak

This essay began as an appreciation to a man I worked with in Binghamton, New York. The original piece ran in the Binghamton Sun Bulletin. Rick lost his life in a collision of a helicopter while covering a news story. His son Eric asked me to send him the essay. Eric has created a website to honor his dad.

The midair collision of two television news he3licopters last week in Phoenix became personal for me when I learned one of the four killed was someone I worked with nearly7 thirty years ago.

Photographer Rick Krolak was one of the four killed while covering a police chase in the city. I worked with Rick when I was a reporter for WICZ-TV in Binghamton back in 1979. Rick was a photographer there who shot and edited my first stories as a TV reporter back in the early days of electronic newsgathering. Our station was among the first in the nation to convert from film to videotape for newsgathering.

Our system included a bulky video camera and a broadcast VCR (video cassette recorder) mounted on a hand truck. It was hardly portable, but the station knew video was the way to go for cost effective pictures of breaking news. Rick helped me understand the equipment limitations, and helped me explore the endless possibilities as a reporter using video as a tool to communicate.

One memorable story was a pre-Memorial Day holiday weekend story about how gas prices might impact vacationers. That story has almost become a cliché in today's news circles, but in 1979 with fuel prices nearing an unheard of ninety-cents a gallon, it was real news.

Another time I recall was when a heavy rain and windstorm hit the Binghamton area in the late afternoon. We both knew the potential of the picture. I jumped behind the wheel of our station news car (a Mercury Comet) and Rick sat in the passenger seat shooting video of the heavy rain and the extensive damage. Through washed out underpasses and intense winds, we got the pictures. We got back in time to edit the story for that night's newscast.

Rick left the station for the greener pastures of WNEP in Wilkes Barre, Pennsylvania that fall. We missed him right away, but knew he was happy at a station with state-of-the-art video equipment, live trucks, and a helicopter. Rick wanted the tools to do his job in the best way possible. Channel 16 provided him with those tools. I spoke to him twice after he left the Southern Tier; then, as what happens with time and new opportunities, we lost contact. He left WNEP a few years later and his career eventually took him to the ABC affiliate in Phoenix.

I'll let the debate over whether news helicopters should be patrolling overhead on news stories be decided among those with vested interests in our right-to-know versus public safety. News coverage judgments must be made with concern over the safety of those covering the news as well as the people making the news.

I was saddened when I heard the news. It's hard to come to terms with the passing of someone who really enjoyed his work and loved his family. He died doing the job he was destined to have. We miss him, but we will move on. Rick would expect us to.

24

Remembering Robert B. Parker

A former television journalist becomes a detective in the mystery novel *Ten Minutes to Air*. The classic 1970's TV detectives and the great mystery writers of my time such as Robert B. Parker inspired the book.

Previously unpublished. I prepared this essay for submission to the Boston Globe. They didn't use it, so I reworked it for this book. I also published a separate appreciation piece on the author of the Spenser mysteries for the Merced Sun Star.

Boston has given us baked beans, the Red Sox, and Spenser. To the people of Boston, thank you for the gift of Robert B. Parker.

I can remember it like it was yesterday. It was the spring of 1988 at my home in western New York State. I was on a doctor-ordered bed rest due to an ailing back. I remember watching a *Today Show* interview of mystery writer Robert B. Parker. Later that day, my wife asked me whether she could get me anything from the store. I told her I didn't need anything from the store, but that if she could go by the library and pick up a Parker novel, I might enjoy reading something from the author I just saw interviewed.

That began a twenty-two year fascination with Parker. Over the years, I devoured the *Spenser* series, embraced the *Jesse Stone* TV-movies with Tom Selleck, rode the range of western romanticism with the anti heroes Virgil and Everett, and sampled any new character he world occasionally try out on his readers.

I gave Parker books as gifts and probably recruited new fans to his work. I even took a stab at the mystery genre myself in 2008 with my reluctant detective Gavin Elliott in *Ten Minutes to Air*. I acknowledge the influence of Parker in my opening pages along with another great writer of mysteries Earl Stanley Gardner.

I welcomed so many things about Parker's literary style. I appreciated the short narrative, the clear (and at times colorful) language, and the no-nonsense main characters that always seemed to have an underlying layer of internal conflict. His books were never too short or too long. I was always comforted by the map of Boston (Spenser's Boston) inside the front and back covers of his go to private eye.

When I chaperoned my fifth grader's class trip to Boston in the early 1990's, I saw the streets described in the Spenser novels. I experienced the atmosphere Robert B. Parker created in his Boston-based stories. The Spenser locales, coupled with a great Red Sox night game, made for a memorable trip.

Robert B. Parker died on the very same day I finished *The Professional*, a Spenser novel that has our protagonist chasing after a blackmailer and eventually investigating three murders. Hawk is there to help in the investigation. Susan resumes her role as sounding board, lover, and soul mate. It wasn't too long and it wasn't too short. For this connoisseur of Parker literature, it was just right.

Time magazine's obituary notes there may be several novels still to be published. I'll be waiting for them. My only hope is the publisher will not seek out a new writer to continue the series. I didn't care for this tactic with *The Godfather* and refused to read the *Gone with the Wind* sequel.

The back problem that saddled me in bed twenty-two years ago has long since disappeared thanks to exercise and watching for the warning signs. But my appetite for Robert B. Parker's body of work will not disappear. He was a habit that will be too hard to break.

The standard Steve Jobs attire
(Photo from Steve Newvine personal collection)

25

Steve Jobs, Broker of Change

At the time of Steve Jobs death, it seemed everyone was writing appreciation essays. I took the assignment with a perspective of not being a consumer of Apple products. This was first published on the website MercedCountyEvents.com

I don't think I'll be able to forget the black turtleneck sweater, blue jeans, wire-rimmed glasses, and stubble beard.

I'm probably the least qualified to weigh in on the life of Apple co-founder Steve Jobs who passed away in early October. I don't own an iPhone or an iPad. I still buy compact disks for my music. And this column is being written on a PC.

But I do agree with many who are beginning to assess Jobs' legacy by putting him in the same league as Henry Ford and Thomas Edison. I could add to that list of Americans who have contributed to the fabric of our commercial existence the likes of Kodak founder George Eastman, and the inventor of the television Philo T. Farnsworth.

For the sake of argument, I concede that none of these inventors brought their ideas forth as pure individual achievements. All worked with people, took ideas established by others, and with the possible exception of Farnsworth, moved their thoughts forward with the help of many individuals. None acted alone.

Edison gave us the light bulb and the phonograph. Ford gave us the assembly line production of the automobile. Eastman put photography into the hands of ordinary people.

Farnsworth gave us the television, but fought bitterly with corporate moguls who tried to marginalize his contributions.

That takes me back to Jobs. He didn't invent the computer, but he and others at Apple Computer did help develop the idea that a computer could be in every home. The company revolutionized the music distribution business with the notion that the consumer could buy just the one song they wanted from an album of ten to twenty cuts. Apple dropped the word computer from its' name and gave us the iPhone which in turn spun several established inventions in a new direction. Even the personal computer, the original idea that launched Jobs and Apple over thirty years ago, was transformed into the lightweight, but heavily technologically driven iPad.

I remember NBC's David Brinkley speaking about the legacy of Elvis Presley at the time of the King of rock and roll's death in the 1970's. "Whether you liked him or not, he changed things. He changed the way, then (1950's) teenage Americans thought about music, clothes, and life."

This thought can be applied to some extent on the legacy of Steve Jobs. He did a lot thinking for us as he brokered ideas and added a few of his own to give the world products they never really knew they wanted or needed.

He may not have been the most compassionate boss. Some have questioned his commitment to corporate responsibility and community service. Several quotes attributed to him are now being discovered as not having been original, but rather quotes he may have borrowed from others without attribution.

But no one will question that he was a brilliant man with a commitment to helping his customers discover they needed something they previously never realized they needed.

He changed things. From the scrapping of traditional business attire at product announcements, to the way all of us think about technology, Steve Jobs changed a lot of things.

Section 7 – Holidays

I love the holiday season. As Halloween passes on to Thanksgiving, I build on the anticipation of the Christmas season.

My Mom told me that as a little girl, Christmas was tough, as her family didn't have a lot of money. She promised herself she would give her family memorable holidays. She did. I hope I'm carrying on the tradition.

Steve's first effort at fiction, a holiday short story

26

Christmas at the Convent

From: Go Where You're Needed (fiction)

Seven o'clock Christmas Eve

By seven P.M., a crowd of about thirty parishioners from Holy Spirit Church gathered in front of the Church entrance. Tom quieted down the group.

"First of all, thank you for coming out tonight," he told the group. "This will mean so much to Sister Loreto. Now, Mom, Dad, and Renee will hand out the song sheets.

The group got their song sheets. Tom had done a pretty good, albeit last minute, job assembling and copying off the words to several Christmas carols.

"We'll sing them in order beginning right now," Tom said. He then led them on their caroling mission.

"Hark the herald angels sing..."

Up the street, the newly formed band of carolers sang out the songs of the holiday.

"Deck the halls with boughs of holly...."

Soon, the door opened. A smiling Sister Margaret Alice, who had been let in on the surprise, gestured her satisfaction as the thirty carolers sang their way into the hallway and living room of the convent. Sitting near a fireplace with a blanket wrapped around her legs, was Sister Loreto. A shut-in this Christmas due to her illness, she was given the gift of music from the Holy Spirit choir.

"Oh come all ye faithful, joyful and triumphant...."

There were tears of joy, hot chocolate for the cold carolers, and lots of love shared on this very special Christmas Eve. There were no regrets about delaying the start of individual family activities on this special night. The group left shortly before eight o'clock and sang carols all the way back to the Church. Everyone was satisfied they made Christmas a little bit brighter for Sister Loreto, the other Sisters, and for themselves.

It was a Christmas Eve to remember.

"Oh holy night, the stars are brightly shining. It is the night of our dear savior's birth."

27

Thanksgiving

Previously unpublished

My fondest memory of Thanksgiving centers on going to my grandmother's house for a traditional dinner. She lived just three miles from our house in nearby Lyons Falls, New York and it seemed we visited her every Sunday. But at Thanksgiving, the trip to her house was real special.

With aunts, uncles, and cousins, I thought we must have had forty people gathered around the two or three tables put together for the big event. Over the years, I've given more serious thought to that early estimate. Maybe it was over twenty people gathered around the table.

The dinners I remember took place in the late 1960's and early 1970's, so the gender roles prior to dinner were fairly distinct for this period in our family history. Women and girls gathered in the kitchen to help Grandma. Men and boys were in the living room watching football or playing cards.

The house was a two-family home with my aunt Cricket, her first husband Jim, and their son Danny living in the other side. Cricket's side of the house became the waiting place for the men and boys in the later years. We'd play cards as we waited for the call from the kitchen that dinner was ready.

At some point around one P.M., everyone was summoned to Grandma's living room where we took our cues from Mom as to where to sit.

The praying of grace before the meal took on a special meaning. When my Grandma Snyder was part of the dinner, she would be asked to lead the prayer. It was longer than the grace we said at home, and with the food steaming before us on the dinner table, it seemed like the prayer would never end. But it would, and we'd eat.

What stood out most for me was what I termed the "Snyder battle of the desserts". Each family was charged with bringing something for the end of the feast. Grandma took care of the basic meal, but dessert was left to her daughters. There were four daughters including my Mom, and each year these women appeared to be secretly trying to outdo their siblings. The rest of us were the beneficiaries of this friendly competition. We had apple and pumpkin pie, cheesecake, tortes, and just about anything you might imagine. The "Snyder battle of the desserts" had no winner, and no loser.

Over the years, the Thanksgiving (and in many years, Easter) dinner remained a true family tradition. As Grandma got older, the dinner location alternated among the aunts and my Mom. The tradition didn't make it into the next generation after my Grandma passed away. I miss that, but I understand how some traditions fade away as other traditions begin.

Still, Thanksgiving at Grandma's house remains a lasting memory of a wonderful time growing up in upstate New York.

28

Holiday Music

Previously unpublished

I can give you a lot of reasons why I like the holiday season. The music, the shopping, the decorations, the wrapping of gifts, the coming together of families, holiday movies, TV specials, church services, food, egg nog, and taking pictures.

I think the holiday season brings out the best in me.

I get sentimental when I begin playing holiday music. My Mom had several Christmas albums when I was growing up and I acquired quite a few in my adult years. I remember the first long-playing vinyl Christmas album she bought: a compilation of various popular artists such as Dinah Shore, Sammy Davis, and Steve Lawrence & Edie Gorme that came from the local *Goodyear Tire* dealer.

I begin celebrating the Christmas season on November 1 with the playing of one vinyl holiday album every day. I play just one album; the album is vinyl. At Thanksgiving, I begin listening to my compact discs of holiday music. Pretty soon, it's all Christmas, all the time in my home, my car, and my workplace.

I always liked the holiday television specials with Andy Williams, Bing Crosby, and others.

When I was about ten years old, I got a cassette recorder for Christmas. For several years following that Christmas, I would produce holiday programs to send to my grandparents who would spend their winters in Florida. My sister Becky would play her electric organ, and my brother Terry would do his Santa impression.

My grandparents enjoyed the holiday programs we would put together. A generation later, I would produce a ten-minute video holiday special featuring my two daughters. They enjoyed that one too.

The anticipation of the holiday cheers me up. The actual holiday keeps my spirits active. I try to keep the momentum going until at least the first day back to work.

Some years, it even lasts longer than that.

Section 8- *Hodge Podge* for $40

The title of this section goes way back to my elementary school days when I would walk home for lunch and watch game shows during the lunch hour. The show Jeopardy debuted in 1964, and while my second grade mind didn't have a chance with the questions and answers, some of the category titles have stayed with me all my life. One of those category titles was *Hodge Podge*.

What follows here are some of my favorite essays that are not necessarily linked to any specific section.

29

Reflections on Two Inaugurations

Previously unpublished. I drew personal comparisons between the inauguration of President Obama in 2008 and President Reagan in 1980.

The inauguration of President Barrack Obama this week gave America and the world the opportunity to look ahead to a future of uncertainty and optimism. Our country faces extraordinary challenges with hardly any easy answers. So this inauguration carries with it so much meaning on so many levels.

While the nation focused on the removal of the race barrier, the call for change, and the promise of hope, I found myself recalling another inauguration that represented a change in direction and hope for a better America.

Twenty-eight years ago, I watched the inauguration of President Ronald Reagan with my wife of eight months from our apartment in Huntsville, Alabama. We had moved there from upstate New York shortly after our wedding so that I could take a new job. The job required working weekends, so that particular January 20th weekday was a day off for me. I spent the whole day glued to the television set.

The international crisis at the moment was the subplot for the big news of the day. This was the day of the release of the American hostages from their 444 days of captivity in Iran. We knew a deal was made to free the captives, but the news of their actual release wasn't confirmed until after the new President was sworn in. In this pre-cable saturated era (CNN was the only cable news source in 1980 and it had been on the air for about a year) our television was tuned to one of the three major networks as it presented the two historic events side by side.

First came the swearing in. Then came the new President's speech. Later in the afternoon, President Reagan announced that the plane carrying the hostages had "cleared Iranian air space". The men and women of the former US embassy staff in Tehran were hostages no more. We had the inauguration a new President and the end to a long international crisis happen on the same day.

Twenty-eight years ago, President Reagan's America faced a huge economic problem. Though many might argue the economic situation of nearly three decades ago was not on the scale of the financial crisis that now seems to have crippled our country, the nation's economy then was mired in high unemployment, rising interest rates and inflation. Candidate Reagan defined the "misery index" (combination of unemployment, inflation and prime interest rates) and made a case for change. His inaugural address, and his actions in those first hours of his new administration, signaled that this would be a new day for the country. It would take another couple of years before the economy was back on track. But we know from those decisive first hours that there would be a new way of doing business in our country.

I listened to the inauguration of President Obama this week on my car radio as a colleague and I drove to the Bay area for a business meeting. The challenges that waited for the new President upon the assumption of his office seemed to grow exponentially from late in the campaign straight through to this historic chain of events leading up to his taking the oath of office. The President has labeled the economy as the new administration's top priority. The international picture will change by the day as the Obama team hits the world stage running. Change has already taken place.

I consider myself to be quite fortunate to have observed two truly historic inaugurations spanning twenty-eight years. We've been through this kind of monumental turn of events before, and our nation was better for having endured it. That turn of events is here right now. We'll get through it. We will grow as a nation. That journey will make us a better people.

30

Watson and the Lack of Gut Instinct

This essay ran in the Merced Sun Star in 2011 after the TV game show Jeopardy! presented a match with two former champions and an IBM computer.

I watched with most of America's *Jeopardy!* fans this week as two top former champions matched wits with IBM's *Watson* computer system in a historic man versus machine competition. It was a real treat to see a celebration of learning as former champs Ken Jennings and Brad Rutter battled Big Blue's best and brightest computer program designers.

While it appeared evident midway through the second night of the competition that *Watson* had the edge in actual knowledge, it was very clear to me that both human contestants knew many of the correct responses. The problem was *Watson's* other strong suit: the computer seemed to have a microsecond advantage with the signaling devices. Watson's signaling device consistently lit up throughout the competition, while we watched Ken and Brad's expressions of frustrations over not being quick enough with their clickers.

While all three contestants were treated equally, the computer was able to shorten the time needed to signal in. The human brain can only react so quickly. The computer is faster. I wish I could say that about my home computer when it's downloading a file.

Watson's knowledge edge was thanks to a room full of several refrigerator size computer stations. The humans could only rely on their brain-sized brains.

But a defining moment occurred in the final *Jeopardy!* round on the Tuesday night program. The category was *US Cities*. The clue was along the lines of "City with two major airports; one named after a WW II Hero and the other after a WW II Battle". Both Ken and Brad had the correct response (Chicago, the airports are O'Hare and Midway). *Watson*'s response was an apparent illogical "Toronto". That was the defining moment. It made a deep impression on me. I would have thought that anyone who didn't know the answer would have at least looked at the category one last time and make a wild guess of some US city. *Any US city*. Any person with a gut instinct might have made a wild guess. *Watson* missed the correct response by a whole country.

While *Watson's* answer didn't hurt the computer's score in the game too much, this *Final Jeopardy*! moment drove home the real lesson of that three-night competition. *Jeopardy!* as in real life, often requires a wild guess, some reasoning, and a willingness to go with your gut. Watson never had a chance in that department.

Who would I want in my corner when an important decision needed to be made? I'll take Ken and Brad or someone of their intellect in the particular area that I needed help. Although the perfect situation would include Ken, Brad, and *Watson* on-call for consultation. That would be a true dream team!

I hope America's children saw the three-night tournament. I hope teachers talked about it in classrooms. And I hope many of our young people were inspired to work hard, study, and maybe consider a field that includes technology.

Jeopardy!'s three-night human versus machine challenge was a special moment for television. It was a morale boosting shot to the men and women at IBM as well as for anyone who works with technology and computers. But at its' very core, the competition was a grand celebration of scholarship, applied knowledge, and the value of a gut instinct.

31

Operation Power Flite

The book *9 From 99* was a travel companion as well as a letter to friends and family back east from Steve's new home in California

The book 9 From 99- Experiences from California's Central Valley was written to tell my family and friends living in New York State that I was doing all right in California, that I have found some interesting things to see out here, and that I have learned a lot about local history. I used California Highway 99 as the focal point of my book about the Golden State. What follows is from the chapter on Merced County and the story about Operation Power Flite.

111

The world of aviation has many milestones. Orville and Wilbur Wright get the lion's share of the credit for their early flights in 1903. Charles Lindbergh became the first to cross the Atlantic in his Spirit of St. Louis. The American space program owes its existence and success to the test pilots who paved the way closer to the nation's entry into space.

Lesser known in the annals of aviation history is the first jet flight to travel around the world without landing for refueling. That milestone flight began at the Castle Air Force Base in Atwater, California.

The year was 1957. The month was January. Dwight Eisenhower was President, Elvis Presley made his third and final appearance on the *Ed Sullivan Show*. (Elvis' three appearances on the Sullivan show were historic given his then record $50,000 fee. The third appearance was on January 6, 1957. His two previous appearances were September 6, 1956 and October 26, 1956) and Humphrey Bogart had just passed away from cancer.

The historic jet flight left Castle on January 16 and returned to California two days later, landing at March Air Force Base in Riverside County. While it was planned to have the mission end where it began at Castle, Merced County was fogged in. (The Tule fog is a weather condition caused by higher relative humidity in the fall and winter months in the Central Valley). The planes had to land in Riverside County.

Five jets began the mission. One left the group on a planned assignment overseas. Another jet would develop mechanical problems and had to land during the flight. With aerial refueling, a flight of three B-52 bombers returned in forty-five hours and nineteen-minutes according to the website bukaska.com. Commanding the flight was Major General Archie Old, Junior.

The mission was called Operation Power Flite (someone in charge of approving the name okayed the variation to the spelling of the word flight). It's successful end made the cover of *Life* magazine.

In *Life* magazine, seven pages of text and photos featured the mission, the crew, and why the flight did not land at Castle. It also called attention to an unusual world record achieved by tail gunner Eugene Preiss. The *Life* article explains that crewman Preiss stayed in his tail gunner position throughout the forty-five hour mission. As the position requires facing backward in the plane, Preiss became the first person to fly around the world backward.

"Operation Power Flite was an important mission in the military history of the Cold War," said Rick Rodriguez, an author and military historian who volunteers at Castle Air Museum. "With the Soviets stirring things up in Europe, it was important for the USA to show it had the capability to counterattack at any time."

The Museum has created a section recognizing Operation Power Flite inside the display area. The section features some of the *Life* photographs and general information.

General Old would achieve the rank of Lieutenant General after Operation Power Flite. He retired in the mid 1960's and lived until 1984. There is a golf course in Riverside County, California named after him. The course is on the site of the former March Air Force Base.

First graders at Elmer Wood Elementary in Atwater, California listen to Steve as a Junior Achievement teacher (Photo:Business Education Alliance of Merced)

32

Learning From Teaching

From MercedCountyEvents.com. Among the non-profit organizations I'm proud to serve in the community, the Business Education Alliance of Merced, or BEAM, has been a real source of satisfaction to me. BEAM is an organization of business people and educators working together to help produce a world-class workforce in Merced County, Callifornia. BEAM is affiliated with the Merced County Office of Education. BEAM also coordinates activities with Junior Achievement, a non-profit organization that matches business people to classrooms to provide real world educational experiences for students.

I have the first graders at Elmer Wood Elementary School in Atwater to thank for giving me a reason to have hope for our future generations.

I presented a Junior Achievement program to Ms Harris' class a few weeks before the end of the school year. Junior Achievement is a national non-profit program designed to provide children of all ages with a better understanding of business and how a strong business sector can help foster stronger and safer communities. The program uses volunteers from the local community. The volunteers come into the classroom armed with a learning "kit" of lesson plans and classroom materials such as posters, handouts, and take home items. The take home items included refrigerator magnets and postcards. After an orientation session, the volunteers are ready to teach the program in classes signed up to the program.

I was a J-A presenter in a second grade class about ten years ago when I lived in upstate New York. I still cherish a group photo presented to me by the class when I finished that five-unit program.

Fast forward ten years to 2011 and I find that not much has changed in how the program is set up and executed. I picked up my learning kit the night before my class. I had to skip any orientation due to the short time frame between signing up and presenting. Fortunately, my previous experience from the 1990's prepared me for what to expect of the program.

I arrived at Elmer Wood School at 7:30 am, signed in at the principal's office, and was directed to the classroom. There, I met twenty smiling faces and Ms Harris. She helped me set up the room with a giant poster of a small community. After giving me an introduction, she sat close by as I began my presentation.

The J-A courses are generally broken down into five sections. Ten years ago, I presented these sections over a five-week period. This time around, I would present all five sections in one three-hour period. Talk about pressure!

The first section dealt with that poster we put up on the wall in front of the class. The students were encouraged to point out things they were familiar with such as a school bus, children, trees, and pets. From this participation exercise, we were able to define a family as a special group of people who may differ in age and relationships but who are connected to one another in some way. We even concluded that different types of family members live in our community and that they all can help one another make it a good place to live.

Part two was about making the distinction between what you need and what you want. Again, there was a lot of class participation as I held up pictures of things we need, such as: healthy food, clothing, and a home; as well as pictures of things we want, such as: an ice cream cone, a video game, and a pet. Some of the students challenged the idea that a pet is a "want" rather than a "need". As a pet owner (our cat Bob has been with us for twelve years), I tend to agree with the kids.

The third unit helped the children define what a job is and why a job is important in helping families acquire their wants and needs. Junior Achievement kits contain workbooks and handouts so that the students can participate in developing their own vision of jobs and career paths. These young people were only six and seven years old, but already they are getting ideas about what they would like to do when they grow up.

Session four was the most active section when I placed a large map of the neighborhood on the floor. The students circled around the map and took turns pointing out such things as a police station, a school building, a hospital, and a fire station. We connected the locations on the maps to the concept of "does this place provide us with a want or a need?" The children enjoyed this session the most. I suspect they enjoyed this the most because they could finally get away from their desks and form a circle around the floor map.

We wrapped it up in the final section with a review of everything covered in the previous four sections and making the point that jobs help families live better lives. I stressed how their hard work in school would eventually earn them a diploma. I then handed out certificates of completion to the group. The certificates were prepared by J-A coordinator Michelle Gonzales in anticipation of a successful completion of the five sessions.

The group was very appreciative of my visit and wished me a safe day as I prepared to leave. I packed up what remained of my Junior Achievement kit, and left the school at the end of the morning.

I really have to hand it to the teachers who are with our children most of the day. They have to be nurturing, firm, and in control throughout the day. Without these key components, the J-A program could not achieve the level of success is has earned over the years.

But I really have to give a shout out to the students. Their attention to the material being presented, their naturally inquisitive nature, and their enthusiasm really made an impact on me. As a volunteer presenter, I got so much out of this group of eager young people.

I'm thankful to work for a company that encourages volunteer opportunities such as Junior Achievement and permits me time away from the regular workday to participate in these activities. I was impressed with the level of support received by the program coordinator in preparing for my day-in-the-classroom. And I was overwhelmed by the dedication to learning I observed in the teacher Ms Harris.

Most of all, I felt honored to be in the presence of our future generation of learners. They are beginning to form ideas about how they can contribute to their communities. They are getting ideas every day about how they might contribute to improving the quality of life when they leave school.

If this first grade class at Elmer Wood Elementary in Atwater is any indication, I think we are in good hands.

They have given me renewed hope in the future.

33

A Friendship Forged in Radio

Originally published in the Merced Sun Star, January 2011

It's funny how you remember some people who dropped along your path in life, people who played a small but important role in shaping the kind of person you hope you became.

One such person was Larry, the guy who taught me how to run an audio board at a small rural radio station back in the mid 1970s.

With one semester under my belt at a community college, the station manager from WBRV in Boonville, N.Y., hired me as a weekend disc jockey. It was for minimum wage, but I saw it as an opportunity I'd dreamed of getting as I pursued my degree in broadcasting.

Larry was only a few years older than me, but he had been with the station about a year since completing a technical school course in radio broadcasting advertised in a magazine.

He showed me everything he knew: how to run the audio board (the machine that controlled all the sources of the audio being broadcast), how to take meter readings on the station transmitter (required by the Federal Communications Commission), and how to be a disc jockey.

He also taught me how to make coffee and showed me where the snow shovels were located. These two skills were necessary for surviving most of those cold and snowy upstate New York winter mornings.

Larry's on-air shift was the afternoon drive, or 3:00 p.m. until the station signed off the air. At that time, most small daytime AM stations had limited hours of operation, unlike today's always on, 24-7 stations. His program was known as "All Request Radio" and listeners were encouraged to call in to request a particular song.

He'd read a long list of dedications following many of the top 40 hits in that era. It was a real lesson watching Larry handle three phone lines that seemed to always be lit up with callers, while at the same time being able to operate the audio board and communicate with his listeners.

The "All Request Radio" format at the station ended when new ownership took over in another year. Larry moved on and would eventually enjoy success in larger radio markets including Utica, Rochester and Albany.

He would later give all that up for a job in marketing and advertising sales at a newspaper in Albany.

I lost track of Larry after he left that small station. We got together once a couple of years later when we both worked in Rochester.

About thirty years later, he called me one day at my Central California home and we picked up where we left off.

From that day forward, we'd exchange e-mail almost weekly, and we would get on the phone about once every three months to talk about everything going on in our lives.

He was a Yankees fan, while I was embracing the world champion San Francisco Giants. He spoke lovingly of his wife Lynn and would tell me about his two stepdaughters, while I'd update him on my wife Vaune and our two daughters.

Both of us had come so far from that small AM radio station where our professional lives began decades ago. Our conversations were carefree, positive, and humorous.

Unfortunately, he would soon learn of a cancer diagnosis and embark on a courageous battle to fight the disease.

Our calls took on a tone of fear masked with optimism. He would detail household projects that he was trying to get accomplished in what I now realize was an effort to get his affairs in order.

He would ask for prayers as he explained what his latest round of treatment would require from him and his family. But he never gave up.

Cancer would eventually take him from his family and friends. His condition worsened during the holiday season and he passed away in mid-January. He was 57.

When I spoke to his wife this week, she directed me to a radio station website that included the obituary and contained dozens of tributes from co-workers, former listeners from his radio career, and neighbors.

It was a great comfort for me to see so many people moved by the news of his passing. I reached out to some former colleagues from that small upstate New York radio station to share the news with them.

I remain grateful that he took the initiative two years ago to reconnect with me. He dropped into my professional life at the very beginning of my working career and then dropped in again a few decades later.

If you made a resolution this year to reconnect with an old friend, let Larry's story be a source of inspiration. It was for me.

34

Grief Ministry With a Nine-Iron

Previously unpublished

He wasn't the easiest man to get to know. His job as the administrator for a government agency put him in a position of deciding how funding to various departments would be allocated. He was tough, fair, but distant. He had to be.

Many who dealt with him wondered whether that toughness extended to his home life. Some would ponder what it must have been like at his family dinner table. If he was half as unyielding at home as he appeared on the job, one could only guess how he handled his children's allowances or problems at school.

But our thoughts about this man changed when one of his three kids died accidentally while away at college. His life changed overnight. Our feelings of anxiety in dealing with him changed overnight as well. We became sympathetic.

My wife and I stood with hundreds of community members in the line leading to the entrance of the funeral home. I promised him at that wake that we could talk after the funeral. He thanked me for the offer. Two weeks later, I thought about making the call. What do you say to a grieving dad? I had no idea, but thinking about that brief conversation at the funeral home, I called him.

"How about a round of golf?" I asked.

"Thanks for the offer, but really, I can't."

"Are you sure? I'm going to play and I would love to have you as company."

He started thinking out loud about the errands he had to do and the time it would take. I told him I could adjust my schedule if that would help.

"Well, I haven't been out in a while. But why not? Sure, I'll join you."

That day, we walked the terrain of a nine-hole executive course. We cursed when our drives would slice off into the woods. We cheered each other as our approach shots landed close to the flag. We grimaced when seemingly easy four-foot putts took us two strokes to land in the cup.

We did not talk much about his loss. I was there to listen and he knew it. But it didn't matter. For those two hours on an afternoon in the sunshine of a brisk fall day in upstate New York, two friends spent time together. We laughed without realizing that for him, it was probably the first laugh he shared with anyone since before the tragedy.

"Thanks for asking me to play," he said as we shook hands at the end of our round.

"Sometimes, I don't know what to say," I answered. "But I do know how to play golf."

Three months later, I left upstate New York for greener pastures and warmer climates in California. He sent me a note that arrived shortly after I started my new life on the west coast.

"Thank you so much for reaching out to me last fall," the note read. *"It meant so much to me."*

And it meant so much to me that I could offer my companionship to a friend in need through the calming influence of an afternoon on the golf course.

35

September 11 at Ten

The Family Flag
(Photo: Steve Newvine personal collection)

From Merced County Events.com, my take on the tenth anniversary of September 11.

We're all looking for words to describe our feelings as the September eleventh tragedy is marked at tenth anniversary ceremonies in New

York, Washington, Pennsylvania, and many communities such as Merced.

I was still looking for words as I prepared this column. What I found were memories of that day that are just as fresh in my mind now as they were ten years ago, writings from a source dating back exactly ten years, and an old American flag.

On that day in 2001, I was at my upstate New York office when a friend of a co-worker called to tell us what had happened. We immediately turned on our radios and began searching for details on the Internet. We did not have television service at our office, so our only real connection to the outside world was through radio and the web. The first picture I saw of the plane hitting the second tower was a still image on the *CNN* website.

Our staff sat around in shock as we saw more pictures, heard more details, and began talking with friends and business associates coming to our office. I was the lead staff person for a committee that was meeting during the lunch hour. None of us at that meeting felt like working or eating. Somehow, we got through the meeting and somehow we got through that workday.

I was also teaching a college course part time and September eleventh was a class day. My class would meet in the late afternoon after my regular workday was finished. I called my department chair Joe Bulsys at the State University of New York College at Geneseo to ask whether the class would meet. If it did meet, I needed some guidance as to how to handle the students who were most likely seeing a day that would be etched in their memory for a lifetime.

Joe told me that the college President had not formally cancelled classes and that I should go to the classroom with no plan to teach that day's lesson. He suggested I tell the students they could leave if they wished, and invite them to remain there and watch the television news coverage along with me in the classroom. About half of the class showed up, and about half of those chose to leave at the beginning of the class period. I stayed with the others for the next hour as we watched the network reports on television.

When I got home at the end of the day, my two teenage daughters were watching the television in our living room. My wife Vaune and I sat with them quietly as the broadcasts continued.

I began keeping a journal in the months following my Mother's death in 2000. I intended to use the journal to write my memories of her and to help me deal with the loss. I located that first journal over the weekend and found that I had an entry dated September 12, 2001. Here's what I wrote:

A day after the tragedy in NYC and Washington. Everyone is shocked by the events. Vaune and I went to church last night where a very beautiful prayer service was held. They burned incense in a pottery bowl throughout the service. To me, it represented the ongoing stream of sadness and pain so many of us were feeling....

Why was there so much pain inflicted on so many people? This is a time of "why us, why now?" I know I don't have an answer and probably will never get an answer. I ask God to help me through this, ..and to touch each family dealing with the loss of loved ones in the bombings.

We have an American flag handed down to us by my wife's grandmother. She came to this country as a young woman from Italy. Her husband worked the coalmines of Pennsylvania and would eventually die before his time from lung disease.

The flag is worn and has some mildew marks from being stored while wet during the years she would fly it in front of her Pennsylvania home. It has forty-eight stars. The reds and blues are not as brilliant as the synthetic flags that are manufactured today. The white has long lost its' sharpness. But my wife and I wouldn't think of putting any other flag in front of our house on those special days when we display it so proudly.

We fly our family heirloom American flag on special occasions every year such as Memorial Day, Flag Day, Veterans Day, and Independence Day. In recent years, we've added September eleventh as a day when that cherished family flag is displayed on our front porch.

We will never forget.

About the author

Steve Newvine is an energy senior program manager working for a public utility. He lives with his wife Vaune in Merced, California. *Microphones, Moon Rocks, and Memories* is his sixth book. He is working on a sequel to his first book *Growing Up, Upstate*, a memoir of his youth in Port Leyden, New York.

Also from Steve Newvine:

GROWING UP, UPSTATE

Memories from Port Leyden, New York including friends, family, and acquaintances that touched the author's life during a special time in our nation's history. $11.00

SOFT SKILLS IN HARD TIMES

15 common sense things you can do to give yourself an advantage at work and in life. $11.00

TEN MINUTES TO AIR

A former TV reporter becomes a suspect in a murder. He becomes a reluctant detective in order to clear his name and find the real killer before he becomes the next victim. Set in upstate New York and inspired by the great television detective shows of the 1970's. **$11.00**

9 FROM 99- Experiences in California's Central Valley

Nine stops along the golden state's historic highway with stories about the people, culture, and spirit of the region. $12.00

GO WHERE YOU'RE NEEDED

A rural community's Christmas season is bittersweet when word that the town's beloved convent will close and the Sisters will soon be leaving. A young man comes home to help save the Convent and learns the true meaning of Christmas. Paperback: $6.00

All books are available at Lulu.com, BN.com (ebook), and Amazon.com, and iTunes/iBooks

Coming in 2012:

Reconnecting with Port Leyden

A continuation of memoirs by Steve Newvine

In this sequel to *Growing Up, Upstate*, Steve Newvine reestablishes contact with friends and acquaintances from his childhood and early adult years when he was a resident of the northern New York village of Port Leyden. Available in November 2012 from: Amazon.com, BarnesAndNoble.com, Lulu.com, and the iBookstore

Made in United States
Orlando, FL
24 October 2025